Sleigh Rides, Jingle Bells, and Silent Nights

UNIVERSITY PRESS OF FLORIDA

Florida A&M University, Tallahassee
Florida Atlantic University, Boca Raton
Florida Gulf Coast University, Ft. Myers
Florida International University, Miami
Florida State University, Tallahassee
New College of Florida, Sarasota
University of Central Florida, Orlando
University of Florida, Gainesville
University of North Florida, Jacksonville
University of South Florida, Tampa
University of West Florida, Pensacola

UNIVERSITY
PRESS OF FLORIDA
Gainesville · Tallahassee · Tampa
Boca Raton · Pensacola · Orlando
Miami · Jacksonville · Ft. Myers
Sarasota

Ronald D. Lankford Jr.

Sleigh Rides Jingle Bells & Silent Nights

A Cultural History of American Christmas Songs

Printed in the United States of America. This book is printed on Glatfelter Natures Book, a paper certified under the standards of the Forestry Stewardship Council (FSC). It is a recycled stock that contains 30 percent post-consumer waste and is acid free.

This book may be available in an electronic edition.

18 17 16 15 14 13 6 5 4 3 2 1

Library of Congress Cataloging-in-Publication Data
Lankford, Ronald D., Jr., 1962–
Sleigh rides, jingle bells, and silent nights : a cultural history of American Christmas songs / Ronald D. Lankford Jr.
pages cm
Summary: The first full examination of popular American Christmas music and its deeper connections to American culture.
Includes bibliographical references and index.
ISBN 978-0-8130-4492-7 (alk. paper)
1. Christmas music—United States—History and criticism.
2. Carols, English—United States—History and criticism. I. Title.
ML2881.U6L36 2013
782.42'17230973—dc23 2013015087

University Press of Florida
15 Northwest 15th Street
Gainesville, FL 32611-2079
http://www.upf.com

To

Elizabeth C. S. Lankford

Contents

Sleigh Rides, Jingle Bells, and Silent Nights

FIGURE 1.1. *White Christmas*, 1954. Rosemary Clooney and Bing Crosby. By permission of Paramount Pictures/Photofest.

1

The American Christmas Song

Our
hit-parade
tunes and our jazz are
quite as representative of our
inner lives as any old ballad is of a
past way of life. As such, these popular
expressions, even though produced by
skillful technicians, are a valuable means
of taking stock of our success or failure in
developing a balanced existence.

Marshall McLuhan, *The Mechanical Bride*

The
way in which
Christmas has been
defined in America reveals
much about our values.

Alan Dundes, *Christmas as a Reflection of American Culture*

Music
has been, is,
and will continue to be an
integral part of our daily lives. It
is vital to our beliefs, our rituals, our
work and our play. It is both a reflection
of and a formative part of the fabric and
needlepoint of our culture and history.

Timothy E. Scheurer, *American Popular Music*, volume 1

In 2006, ASCAP (the American Society of Composers, Authors and Publishers) released a list of the top twenty-five most popular Christmas songs from the previous five years.[1] While the list didn't include every popular holiday song (it included only songs published by ASCAP), it did offer a good snapshot of the kinds of songs that have sustained popularity with American listeners. What was perhaps most surprising at the time was how little the holiday song market had changed in sixty to seventy years: familiar Christmas classics, both in their original and rerecorded versions, dominated the list. Seventeen of the twenty-five songs were first introduced between 1934 and 1954; another five between 1955 and 1964. One song, the "Carol of the Bells," has multiple origins—popular lyrics were added in 1947 to the 1904 Ukrainian composition. The two "newer" songs date from 1970 and 1984.

Several songs remain popular in versions by their original performers. Bing Crosby, for instance, remains on the ASCAP list with "White Christmas" (#5), Gene Autry with "Rudolph the Red-Nosed Reindeer" (#10), and Nat King Cole with "The Christmas Song" (#1). Bobby Helms continues to be associated with "Jingle Bell Rock" (#6) and Brenda Lee with "Rockin' Around the Christmas Tree" (#14). The original version of "The Little Drummer Boy" (#8) by the Harry Simeone Chorale and Orchestra remains the most popular as does Burl Ives's version of "Holly Jolly Christmas" (#18), Andy Williams's "It's the Most Wonderful Time of the Year" (#11), and José Feliciano's "Feliz Navidad" (#15). From "White Christmas" in 1942 to "Feliz Navidad" in 1970, these songs represent a rich mine of Christmas music history that remains, to millions of listeners, contemporary.

Newer versions of these classic Christmas songs, versions recorded later than the original issue or hit, are equally represented

FIGURE 1.2. Nat King Cole, ca. 1947. Black and white negative. Gottlieb Collection, Library of Congress.

on the ASCAP list. Most of these, however, were versions recorded before the time period in question, 2001–2005. In other words, while many of these rerecorded songs are newer than the original versions, they nonetheless qualified as older, favored versions of classic Christmas songs that have remained popular.

The Pretenders' "Have Yourself a Merry Little Christmas" (#2), the Eurythmics' "Winter Wonderland" (#3), Madonna's "Santa Baby" (#25), and John Mellencamp's "I Saw Mommy Kissing Santa Claus" (#20) were all issued in 1987 on *A Very Special Christmas* (one of a series of compilations that raised money for Special Olympics). Elvis Presley's "Blue Christmas" (#16) and "Here Comes Santa Claus" (#22) date from 1957, while the Ronettes' "Sleigh Ride" (#9) dates from 1963.

While the ASCAP list evinces a strong connection to yesteryear, it also reveals a less tangible result: these songs, in both old and new versions, remain vital to the American celebration of Christmas. Americans, the list suggests, cannot imagine celebrating Christmas without their favorite holiday songs performed by their favorite singers: without "Blue Christmas" and Elvis, without "White Christmas" and Bing Crosby, it would not be, to millions of Americans, officially Christmas.

Why did these songs play such a vital role within an American Christmas during the 1940s and 1950s, and why do they (especially since the 1980s) continue to evoke nostalgia for a lost time and place today? Perhaps the most obvious reason—though a reason that clarifies little—is that we simply like Christmas songs and have gotten into the habit of listening to them from Thanksgiving to New Year's. Many of us have grown up within a Christmas tradition or a culture that places great importance on that tradition, making it difficult to avoid holiday music, even if we wished to do so. As children, we listened to our parents' favorite holiday albums—perhaps Johnny Mathis's *Merry Christmas* (1958), the Vince Guaraldi Trio's *A Charlie Brown Christmas* (1965), or Alabama's *Christmas* (1982)—and later passed along these very same LPs, now CDs or downloads, to our own children or nephews and nieces. Listening to these holiday albums makes us feel good, reminding us of earlier Christmas memories with family and friends and linking us to both the past and the present. Because we know popular Christmas music as well as we know any music, we can join in the spirit of the season as we hum along, or we can escape into the warm envelope of nostalgia for simpler places and times.

The American connection to Christmas songs, however, runs much deeper than habit and feeling good. By expressing so many aspects of our holiday experience, Christmas songs also reflect American values, ideals, and desires; values, ideals, and desires that were born in the nineteenth century and streamlined in the 1940s and 1950s, and which many attempted to renew during the 1980s and beyond. Working like shorthand, the modern holiday song gives voice to the Christmases we celebrate and those we wish to celebrate. Resting beneath the surface of jolly Santas, winter wonderlands, and roasting chestnuts is an intricate and at times disjointed cultural landscape crowded with the meanings of a modern American Christmas. The songs that most readily evoke those meanings, desires, and anxieties have become classics, songs that Americans listen to year after year because the myths and ideas they represent are part of our mental landscape.

As a reflection of American values and desires, the Christmas song is both multifaceted and endlessly conflicted. On the surface, the idea that the Christmas song is conflicted seems wrong. As a Coca-Cola ad from 1944 stated, "The spirit of good will rules the Christmas season."[2] Surely everyone can embrace the joy that Santa brings, bask in the warm glow of childhood holiday memories, and share the excitement of caroling and decorating a Christmas tree. Besides, modern secular Christmas songs are, for the most part, *happy,* celebrating the spirit of the season in an affirmative fashion. People listen to Christmas songs because they make everyone feel joyful, not conflicted and confused.

Beneath the surface, however, the American Christmas song is a much thornier hybrid than we imagine. And this paradox has always been and remains true, even when returning to the supposedly more placid days of the 1940s and 1950s when many of these songs first appeared. Underneath visions of winter scenes by Currier and Ives in "Have Yourself a Merry Little Christmas," a dark nostalgia longs for a yesterday that can never be regained. On the flipside of Santa's much-anticipated arrival in "Here Comes Santa Claus" looms an army of advertisements, salespersons, and mall displays. While shoppers embrace the abundance and goodwill of the season in "Pretty Paper," they are also reminded of the tired, hungry, and lonely who remain social outsiders. Every warm memory has a lonely echo; every well-chosen present, a bill of sale.

Americans would like to spend more time with family and friends in the sanctity of the home ("I'll Be Home for Christmas") but are required to enter the public space of the market as workers, shoppers, and creditors ("Santa Claus Is Comin' to Town"); Americans wish to reward themselves for another year of hard work with the sensual and social pleasures of feasts, parties, and casual gatherings ("Rockin' Around the Christmas Tree"), while also contributing generously to favorite charities and dropping loose change into the Salvation Army bucket ("If

We Make It Through December"). While Americans wish to embrace the ebullient and easygoing mood of the holiday, decorating the Christmas tree while sharing a glass of eggnog ("It's the Most Wonderful Time of the Year"), they often find themselves wondering whether the Christmas season—filled with rich food, multiple gifts, and excessive busyness—is *too* much ("Grandma Got Run Over by a Reindeer").

Holiday songs have served as reminders of these overlapping ideals while allowing a cultural framework for Americans to negotiate conflicts and differences. The process, however, is perhaps an unconscious one. Because Americans have lived with these songs and their contradictory messages for such a long time, it is easy to overlook how intricately they reflect the culture of Christmas. Beneath the familiar melodies and words, Christmas songs reveal a portrait of the American psyche past and present, wishing simultaneously to embrace nostalgia, commerce, charity, carnival, romance, and travesty.

The first theme to emerge in the modern Christmas song was nostalgia. Songs like "White Christmas" (1942), "Have Yourself a Merry Little Christmas" (1944), and "The Christmas Song (Merry Christmas to You)" (1946) connected with listeners by offering wistful images of the American past. Against the historical backdrop of sudden change in the early twentieth century, nostalgia-tinged songs offered a bridge for those who felt disconnected from preindustrial America. Images of snow and roasting chestnuts also provided Americans a brief respite from shopping for gifts and the pressures of a modern Christmas.

Holiday songs focusing on children and Santa Claus surfaced at nearly the same time as those focusing on nostalgia. In a sense, the gifts that arrived with "Here Comes Santa Claus" (1947) and

"Rudolph the Red-Nosed Reindeer" (1949) more closely represented the post–World War II American zeitgeist. As a robust economy promised to lift all boats, America expanded into a consumers' republic. Because these songs were children's songs, however, they provided psychological cover for middle-class parents: materialism is only embraced indirectly through the benevolent Santa Claus.

By the late 1940s, nostalgia and Santa Claus had to make room for other kinds of Christmas song categories. Songs focusing on the holiday blues and hard times reminded Americans that while many enjoyed the emotional and material fruits of the season, others were alone, financially strained, and in need of charity. Songs like Ernest Tubbs's version of "Blue Christmas" (1949) underlined the melancholy side of Christmas loneliness, while Willie Nelson's "Pretty Paper" (1963) explored issues of charity and class. While all of these songs had roots in Charles Dickens's *A Christmas Carol* (1843), each writer Americanized the message.

Other holiday song categories were perhaps—on the surface—more at odds with mainstream American culture. The carnival strain in the Christmas song had deep roots in pre-Christian winter festivals but would emerge in the mainstream as romantic fare like "Winter Wonderland" (1934), "Let It Snow! Let It Snow! Let It Snow!" (1945), and "Baby, It's Cold Outside" (1949). While the carnival tradition had viewed the holiday as an excuse for sensual abandon, these songs more conservatively focused on romance and, on occasion, no more than the suggestion of sex. Interestingly, none of these songs even mentioned Christmas.

Another strain of holiday song—satire—attempted to break all the rules, turning Christmas tradition on its head. While often dismissed as novelty, songs like Yogi Yorgesson's "I Yust Go

Nuts at Christmas" (1949), Elmo and Patsy's "Grandma Got Run Over by a Reindeer" (1979), and Weird Al Yankovic's "Christmas at Ground Zero" (1986) were intended as social critiques. These songs seemingly rejected part or all of the American Christmas experience by transforming the familiar symbols of the holiday into travesties.

It would be tempting to view Christmas songs focusing on charity, carnival, and satire as critical of American prosperity following World War II. For instance, the homeless man in "Pretty Paper" suggests that the bountiful American system has somehow failed. These nonmainstream categories, however, were less about rejecting the postwar boom than negotiating boundaries. Charity offered a safety net for those who had not yet obtained their slice of the American pie; carnival offered nothing more than a temporary reprieve from social boundaries; and satire merely pointed out pretension and hypocrisy with an eye on reform. Only a rowdy few wanted to do away with Christmas. Everyone else wanted to make it live up to its humanistic promise and the democratic impulse.

It is easy when considering these different categories to view the American holiday song as representing a smorgasbord of disparate values. On the surface, "White Christmas" and "Grandma Got Run Over by a Reindeer" have nothing in common. Even with vast differences, a larger touchstone underpinned all of these categories: home and family. Building on the values supported by the middle class during the nineteenth century, Americans refined the idea of a domestic Christmas through holiday songs during the 1940s and 1950s. The centrality of family and home in the Christmas song was complicated, however, by another touchstone: holiday gifts. While Santa Claus relieved parental guilt over spoiling children, accelerated holiday spending placed increased pressure on family members who paid the bills. Family and home remained most central to the Christmas song (and the Christmas experience), but it was difficult to separate families and homes from an abundance of consumer goods.

Christmas Music Past

Even before Charles Dickens's *A Christmas Carol* in 1843, Christmas culture emerged as an essential part of the nascent middle-class experience in America. During the same time period, there was also a renewed interest in Christmas carols and songs. In America, a number of new carols were written, including "It Came upon a Midnight Clear" (1849), "We Three Kings of Orient Are" (1857), and "Away in a Manger" (1885). Likewise, a number of favorite secular songs were penned, including "Jingle Bells" (1857), "Jolly Old Saint Nicholas," and "Up on the House Top" (the latter two were probably written between the Civil War and the turn of the twentieth century). While these songs were widely known, they were performed at home on the family's piano or in church by choirs. In the nineteenth century, listening to music meant listening to live music.

This would change quickly and radically during the twentieth century, thanks to the development of mass media. Instead of hearing Christmas songs in church and performing them at home, Americans would listen to holiday songs on records (at home and on jukeboxes), at the movies, and on the radio. The history of the popular Christmas song is wrapped up in the emergence of new technology that allowed millions of Americans to buy copies of Bing Crosby's "White Christmas" and the King Cole Trio's "The

FIGURE 1.3. Thomas Nast, "Christmas Station," ca. 1889. Wood engraving. Library of Congress.

Christmas Song." The holiday song, performed by a well-known singer, pressed on a 78rpm record, and sold on the mass market, would create a new category of popular music.

Also of note, the Christmas song that became popular during the 1930s and 1940s was, by and large, a secular affair. While the older carols continued to be recorded, religion had been stripped from hits like "Have Yourself a Merry Little Christmas," "Winter Wonderland," and "Rudolph the Red-Nosed Reindeer." Although new carols were composed, such as "The Little Drummer Boy" and "Do You Hear What I Hear?," these songs were rare exceptions.

Depending on who is relating the history, the popular Christmas song as Americans know it today dates back only to the 1930s or 1940s. There are known recordings of Christmas songs as far back as 1902, but a scratchy version of "Jingle Bells" sung by a barbershop quartet is hardly what we think of when considering modern Christmas songs.[3] And while a number of early attempts at recording holiday material were popular in their day, such as narrations by Gilbert Girard and Harry Humphrey during the early 1920s, they failed to create lasting cultural traditions.[4] That leaves us with two likely popular Christmas song trajectories that overlap but are nonetheless, I believe, reconcilable.

Billboard author Joel Whitburn contends in *Christmas in the Charts* that the holiday song received its proper start in 1934. "This timeline of Christmas/Holiday songs begins in 1934, when two standards ["Winter Wonderland" and "Santa Claus Is Comin' to Town"] were introduced after a long drought of fresh new holiday songs. These two 1934 tunes ushered in the golden era of wonderful secular holiday songs."[5] Guy Lombardo's version of "Winter Wonderland" and George Hall's version of "Santa Claus Is Comin' to Town" both became popular in 1934. In *The Christmas Carol Reader,* William Studwell also points out that "Santa Claus Is Comin' to Town" (originally written in 1932) was the first in the golden age of American Christmas songs. Between 1932 and 1951, nineteen classics, including "It's Beginning to Look a Lot Like Christmas," "Sleigh Ride," and "Silver Bells," became the bedrock of our popular Christmas songs.[6]

The Whitburn and Studwell origin story, however, has a couple of glitches. No Christmas recordings of the 1930s came close to selling the number of copies that "White Christmas," "The Christmas Song," and "Rudolph the Red-Nosed Reindeer" would sell during the 1940s (and Whitburn's reference to a "long drought" is misleading: there had never been a glut of holiday songs in the newer style during the 1920s). Dave Marsh and Steve Propes offer that "Prewar America still insisted on taking Christmas straight."[7] A more tangible issue may have been the Depression (1929–1941). Author Tim Hollis notes that "'Santa Claus Is Comin' to Town' first appeared in 1934, but it originally had a little touch of irony in that it seemed to reflect an impossible dream for those struggling with the Great Depression at the time."[8] Songwriters and singers may have directed more attention toward the Christmas song during the 1930s than in the past, but a slumping economy and poor record sales seemed to dampen the potential for holiday recordings.

Marsh and Propes offer a slightly different history of the American Christmas song in *Merry Christmas, Baby.* "As far as modern Christmas music is concerned, Santa Claus arrived in 1942."[9] To the authors, the arrival of Santa Claus refers to the appearance of "White Christmas" on both the pop charts and the Harlem Hit Parade in October and November of 1942. Important changes had occurred between the issue of "Santa Claus Is Comin' to Town" in 1934 and "White Christmas" in 1942. During the eight-year interval, the Depression had ended and Americans had entered World War II. More important, however, was the new centrality of the record/recording itself along with the music industry's realization that holiday music would actually sell. "'White Christmas' changed Christmas music forever," write Marsh and Propes, "both by revealing the huge potential market for Christmas songs and by establishing the themes of home and nostalgia that would run through Christmas music evermore."[10]

Considering both histories, the years between 1934 and 1942 can be seen as the development of an idea: Christmas songs had the potential to be more than novelty tunes played during a short space of time for one season and then forgotten; Christmas songs had the potential to be more than an advertisement for sheet music sales.[11] At first, no one within the music industry imagined the possibility of sales for successful holiday songs. Noting the pre-1942 view of the Christmas song, *Billboard* wrote, "Most Tin Pan Alley tunesmiths avoid laboring over holiday songs because previous experiences had convinced them that the tunes are generally played on that day alone and the copies of sheet music are cleared off the retail counters the day after."[12] Between 1934 and 1941, newly minted Christmas songs like "Santa Claus Is Comin' to Town" and "Winter Wonderland" only waited for the right singer, a livelier arrangement, and a better economy to realize their potential.

With the release of "White Christmas" in 1942, the potential that no one had imagined became a reality. The trend accelerated after the war thanks to a booming American economy and population. The record industry, seemingly displaced by radio during the

1930s, rebounded. "By 1945, record sales climbed to $109 million," writes LeRoy Ashby in *With Amusement for All*, "far above the $5.5 million during the Depression's low point."[13] Multimillion sellers like "White Christmas" played an essential part in these growing sales. In a ten-year period, Bing Crosby's version of "White Christmas" sold nine million records.[14] With an avalanche of sales and favored holiday songs that continued to chart and sell in large quantities for successive years, the Christmas song had arrived.

The arrival of the holiday song also gave witness to the consolidation of a national Christmas culture. The Macy's Thanksgiving Day Parade, immortalized in *Miracle on 34th Street* (1947), was founded in 1924, while the national tree lighting was established by President Calvin Coolidge in 1928. In 1937, Charles W. Howard established the first Santa Claus school, working to institute standards for the profession. In the early 1940s, the president and Congress moved Thanksgiving to the fourth Thursday in November instead of the last, adding precious shopping days to the season. As the Great Depression came to a close and Crosby's "White Christmas" climbed the charts, the national holiday culture was set to expand as never imagined.

Sacred or Secular?

As noted earlier, one aspect of the new Christmas song was clear: it was primarily a secular affair. Following "White Christmas" in 1942, "I'll Be Home for Christmas" (1943), "Have Yourself a Merry Little Christmas" (1944), "Let It Snow! Let It Snow! Let It Snow!" (1945), and "The Christmas Song" and "Christmas Island" (1946) became popular. During these same years, neither carols nor newly written sacred material experienced a similar surge. The dominance of secular songs would likewise be mirrored on the

ASCAP Top Twenty-Five list sixty years later: only one song on the ASCAP list, "The Little Drummer Boy," could be considered religious. When it came to record sales and chart activity, Christmas songs, not carols, were the clear winners.

Carols, however, continued to be recorded and issued, and have often been included as B-sides (on 78s and later on 45s), album tracks (on 33⅓ LPs), and as CD tracks. Bing Crosby's version of "Silent Night" sold well in 1935, and in 1947 Decca issued a new version of "White Christmas" with "God Rest Ye Merry Gentlemen" on the flipside. On occasion, new holiday songs with religious themes, such as "Do You Hear What I Hear?" (1962), became popular.

The strength of carols is also reflected in how many times they have been recorded. In *Christmas in the Charts: 1920–2004*, Joel Whitburn includes a list titled "Top 100 Christmas/Holiday Songs." Here, Whitburn does not consider sales or hits, but only the number of times each song was included on an album. By using this method, we learn that despite the total sales of popular songs like "White Christmas" (#2) and "Rudolph the Red-Nosed Reindeer" (#19), many religious songs received equal billing within the grouping of album tracks. Within the top ten we find "Silent Night" (#1), "O Holy Night" (#4), "O Come All Ye Faithful" (#6), "The First Noel" (#8), and "Joy to the World" (#9).

One might easily divide Christmas music into two categories: Christmas songs (secular) and carols (sacred). Noting the emergence of the recorded Christmas song, Marsh and Propes write, "There may have been a time, before the birth of the record industry, when all Christmas music was religious music. But at least since the start of the record age, the musical component of the season has been as much secular as spiritual."[15] This split between

FIGURE 1.4. Gertrude Käsebier, "The Manger," 1901. Glass negative, 8 × 10. Library of Congress.

sacred and secular holiday songs also mirrors a common conundrum over Christmas and the values associated with the holiday: the clash between Christian beliefs and materialism. "Indeed, there are two Christmases: a cultural Christmas, and a religious or Christian Christmas," observes Bruce David Forbes in *Christmas: A Candid History*. "Some people focus on one, some focus on the other, and many are involved in both."[16] This split epitomizes a central dichotomy in American Christmas celebrations: the disparity between a secular and a sacred Christmas and the struggle between a commercial and a noncommercial Christmas.

The popular view of this divide seems to have been born out of the haphazard historical development of Christmas: one of Christianity's most important holy days coincides with the retail sector's most important shopping season. Christians place their emphasis on the birth of Christ, goodwill, and charity; businesses prefer to emphasize the role of Santa Claus and gift-giving.

Within the Christmas song, the perceived split between the secular and sacred Christmas was sometimes made obvious. When the holiday long player album became a possibility in 1948 (with the 33⅓ format), performers often divided the A- and B-sides between secular and religious material. When Gene Autry formed his own label during the 1950s and recorded an album titled *Rudolph the Red-Nosed Reindeer* (1957), the first half included songs about Rudolph and Santa Claus, while the second side featured traditional carols. Johnny Mathis's *Merry Christmas* (1958) offered a slight variation, splitting the secular and sacred with the exception of inserting the quieter "Silver Bells" among carols. Even on a mostly instrumental album like *Christmas with Chet Atkins* (1961), the first half of the album included "Jingle Bell Rock" and "White Christmas" while side B included traditional carols and "The Little Drummer Boy." This style of division, however, seems to have been mostly lost with the emergence of the compact disc; without clearly divided album sides, all tracks run together.

Perhaps more common than dividing carols and songs, many performers sprinkled both sacred and secular material throughout an album in no particular order. The Vince Guaraldi Trio's *A Charlie Brown Christmas* (1965) included "What Child Is This?" and "Hark, the Herald Angels Sing" along with the "Linus and Lucy" theme; Willie Nelson's mostly secular *Pretty Paper* (1979) includes "Silent Night" and "O Little Town of Bethlehem"; and five of the fifteen songs on Bob Dylan's *Christmas in the Heart* (2009) are carols.

Despite the perceived split between Christmas songs and carols on many holiday albums and the broader split within American culture, it has become easy to question the relevance of religion to a modern Christmas. Most of the Christmas songs written since "White Christmas" in 1942 are secular, especially those that have become popular. Even during the 1950s James H. Barnett argued that traditional carols were being pushed aside. "The mass media of entertainment place a heavy premium on novelty, and this lures song writers to grind out new Christmas songs each year. . . . This ensures a constant supply of new Christmas songs, which seem about to displace the older, traditional ones."[17]

Forbes updated Barnett's commentary in 2007. "If you examine the store racks featuring CDs of Christmas music today, they will include some CDs with a sacred focus and some with a few religious songs mixed in among commercial secular songs, but the vast majority of the selections, in jazz, country, rock, and a wide range of other styles, are songs about the cultural experience of Christmas."[18] And while carols have not been completely displaced, it is clearly the secular songs that have remained most popular and that continued to return to the charts in both original and newer versions.

This displacement of carols by Christmas songs also follows the larger development within American holiday culture. "Religion has not played an important role in the emergence of the modern form of the celebration," notes William B. Waits in *The Modern Christmas in America*. "This may come as a surprise—even a shock—to those who think of Christmas as being predominantly religious. However, in practice, the secular aspects of the celebration, such as gift giving, the Christmas dinner, and the gathering of family members, have dwarfed its religious aspects in resources spent and concern given."[19] Karal Ann Marling concurs in *Merry Christmas!*: "[T]he American Christmas has always been more secular than sacred."[20]

While the residue of the Gospels remains in a song like "Pretty Paper" (1963), and the concept of good will pervades many modern Christmas songs, these concepts are never specifically Christian. Indeed, Charles Dickens's *A Christmas Carol* (1843), perhaps the most influential source on the importance of charity within the holiday celebration, mostly avoids religion. While Christian ideals continued to permeate the American holiday experience, their influence had dwindled greatly by the 1940s and 1950s.

A Realignment of Christmas Values

While reducing the effect of religion within an American Christmas disassembles a familiar and perhaps comfortable dualism, it presents us with a new dilemma over how we—as individuals and as a culture—define the meaning of Christmas. Seemingly, removing a contentious component would simplify the process. Far from simplifying our understanding of Christmas, however, the reduction of religion introduces other contradictions and conflicts. And even in a nondominant position, religion continues to compete among other belief systems. In essence, without the sacred-secular divide providing broad guidelines for understanding multiple Christmas values, a plethora of lesser values would be allowed to compete on an even playing field.

This apparent complexity, however, might be resolved by learning to look at Christmas culture from a fresh perspective; we have viewed holiday values through sacred-secular lenses for so long that everything appears fuzzy when we first remove them. By focusing more closely on the Christmas song (and popular holiday culture in general), it becomes clear that certain ideals and beliefs reoccur more often, that certain concepts mean more than others. Home and family, as noted earlier, weigh heavily in the holiday balance, as do the prospect of gifts and the need for charity. This opens the possibility—when considering the Christmas song of the 1940s and 1950s—of discovering a new pattern, perhaps one that replaces the split between religion and consumption.

Likewise, the possibility remains that Americans continue to see many aspects of Christmas as sacred, even when these aspects do not fall under the auspices of traditional religion. The Christmas song, along with other popular culture responses to the modern holiday, may represent more than a falling away from tradition, more than acquiescence to commercial culture. Written against a backdrop of a rich holiday heritage but adjusted for the modern era, the possibility remains that these songs reflect a realignment of Christmas values.

FIGURE 2.1. Thomas Nast, "Christmas Eve," ca. 1889. Wood engraving. Library of Congress.

PLATE 1. "Santa Claus Has Gone to War," ca. 1942–1943. Photomechanical print. National Archive.

PLATE 2. S. D. Ehrhart, "On Earth Peace, Good Will Toward Men," 1908. Photomechanical print: offset, color. Library of Congress.

PLATE 3. "For Liberty and Peace on Earth Give War Bonds," 1941–1945. Photomechanical print. National Archives.

PLATE 4. "The Night Before Christmas, or, Kriss Kringle's Visit," 1858. General Collection, Beinecke Rare Book and Manuscript Library, Yale University.

PLATE 5. Denver Gillen, "Rudolph the Red-Nosed Reindeer," ca. 1939. Rauner Special Collections Library at Dartmouth.

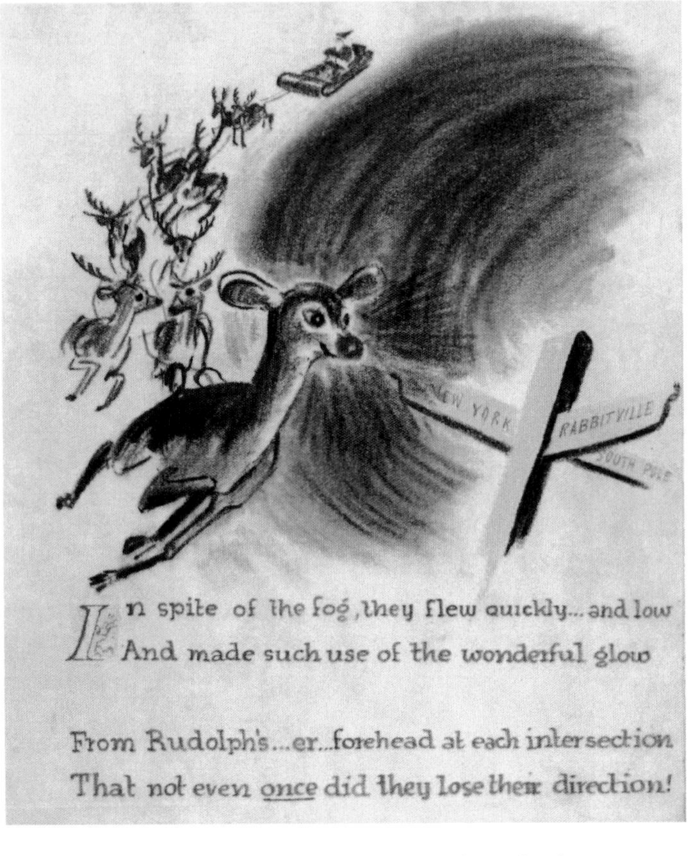
NEW YORK
RABBITVILLE
SOUTH POLE
In spite of the fog, they flew quickly... and low
And made such use of the wonderful glow
From Rudolph's...er...forehead at each intersection
That not even once did they lose their direction!

PLATE 6. Denver Gillen, "Rudolph the Red-Nosed Reindeer," ca. 1939. Rauner Special Collections Library at Dartmouth.

PLATE 7. Frank A. Nankivell, "Puck Christmas 1902," 1902. Print: chromolithograph. Library of Congress.

PLATE 8. Frank A. Nankivell, "Puck Christmas 1904," 1904. Print: chromolithograph. Library of Congress.

2

Nostalgia: Home for Christmas

Some
recalled the tinkle
of bells on bright winter
mornings, after snow, when
the sleighs came out.

Lloyd Morris, *Postscript to Yesterday*

We need
only reflect on the
character of our aesthetic
experience, on how often the poem,
the story, the song, the picture
"reminds us of" or "captures exactly"
the way we felt then or "makes us feel
sad for some lovely time and place we
shall never see again."

Fred Davis, *Yearning for Yesterday*

DURING THE 1940S, "White Christmas" would set the stage for a number of classic American holiday songs steeped in a misty longing for yesteryear. The lyrics of "White Christmas" were less concerned with capturing the realistic details of past Christmases than providing a vague outline of favored traditions and memories filled with nostalgia. "'White Christmas' had established a new seasonal theme," write Dave Marsh and Steve Propes, "the longing for the comforts of home and the way things used to be (whether or not they'd ever actually been quite so pacific and pastoral as memory claimed)."[1] After all, the song's author, Irving Berlin, and its first singer, Bing Crosby, were *dreaming* of a white Christmas. And it was a beautiful dream that floated wistfully on the radio airwaves, allowing listeners the indulgence of adding their own memories to the melancholy mix.

"White Christmas" also ushered in a new era in relation to how Christmas would be explored and exploited within popular American culture.[2] Before 1942, Christmas songs and movies appeared sporadically, and a number, as with Crosby's recording of "Silent Night" in 1935, were popular. But before the success of "White Christmas" and the movie the song appeared in, *Holiday Inn* (1942), the popular cultural industry had not viewed the themes of home and hearth, centered on the Christmas holiday, as a unique market.[3] Likewise, no one seems to have considered that Christmas-themed songs and movies could be recycled Christmas after Christmas, reappearing on *Billboard* and box office charts.

These changes were also mirrored in the development of other popular culture products. The winter-themed paintings of folk artists would be mass-marketed as greeting cards in the mid-1940s and beyond. Beginning in 1946, Hallmark would sell millions of holiday cards featuring the paintings of Grandma Moses.

Christmas had long been a central part of American life; the modern media, however, would disperse this nostalgic vision of the holiday simultaneously to millions of Americans. Radio, records, movies, and greeting cards worked to generate an updated version of a Currier and Ives Christmas.

Sung by Crosby, "White Christmas" first hit the airwaves in 1942 and also circulated widely in *Holiday Inn* (August 1942), starring Crosby and Fred Astaire. Beginning in October, "White Christmas" would remain on the *Billboard* chart for seventeen weeks, ten of those at number one; "White Christmas" would also reach number seven on the Harlem Hit Parade.[4] The broad appeal of "White Christmas" would be followed by similar holiday recordings over the next several years, exploring the themes of home and nostalgia. In 1944 Judy Garland offered "Have Yourself a Merry Little Christmas," a song featured in *Meet Me in St. Louis* (November 1944). Mel Tormé and Bob Wells would pen "The Christmas Song (Merry Christmas to You)" the same year, but the song would not become a hit until the King Cole Trio recorded it in 1946. All of these songs have remained popular, all have been recorded by many performers, and all were steeped in a nostalgic longing for a simpler time somewhere in the undefined American past.

Writers have noted the difficulty of pinning down the meaning of contemporary nostalgia. Originally, nostalgia was defined by physicians as a longing for home, a feeling most commonly experienced by soldiers serving in distant lands. Contemporary nostalgia, however, might be described as the past fondly remembered, as personal memory, primarily disassociated from anything unpleasant. At the beginning of Booth Tarkington's *The Magnificent Ambersons* (1918), the narrator recalls an earlier period when life seemingly moved at a slower pace. "In the days before deathly contrivances hustled them through their lives, and when they had no telephones—another ancient vacancy profoundly responsible for leisure—they had time for everything: time to think, to talk, time to read, time to wait for a lady!"[5] Engaged in warm recollection, the narrator leaves the impression of wishing to return to an earlier place and time.

But nostalgia is complicated by its relationship to the present. A fond memory may also be tinged by wistfulness, as though to say the present, when measured against the past, is somehow lacking; that to express *people were different back then and they really cared about their neighbors* is also to say *people care less about their neighbors today*. In this way, nostalgia works as a running commentary on the present. One can find traces of this nostalgic mood in author Helen Bartlett Bridgman's description of an old-fashioned Christmas in *Within My Horizon* from 1920. "Human nature is said to be much the same the world over, yet the shining eyes of those New England children looking up into that tree, a tree taken only a few hours before from the woods near by, did realize a certain ideal. To them Christmas with its good cheer and simple tokens was a vital, exquisite thing. Modern city children, with their little old heads, their almost uncanny appraisement of values, miss so much, so much."[6] When the past is compared to the present, observes Fred Davis in *Yearning for Yesterday*, present circumstances "are invariably felt to be, and often *reasoned* to be as well, more bleak, grim, wretched, ugly, derivational, unfulfilling, frightening, and so forth."[7]

While we generally think of nostalgia as an emotion experienced by individuals, Davis also speaks of a broader social nostalgia. In the wake of sudden social changes and historic events, millions of people may experience disruption, "creating fertile social psychological medium for the production and diffusion of nostalgic sentiment."[8] The central element here is sudden change. "It is as if at the moment of recognizing the *new* situation or condition we are led to remark to ourselves and to others, 'Hey, isn't this a lot different from what was being seen/said/thought/felt just a few short years ago?'"[9] In twentieth-century American history, it would be easy to point to a number of broader social events qualifying as "sudden social changes," including World Wars I and II, the Great Depression, the assassination of John F. Kennedy, the youth upheaval of the 1960s, the oil and economic crises of the 1970s, and the attacks on the World Trade Center in 2001.

As "White Christmas" was issued in 1942, part of America's melancholy mood and longing for the past was easy to understand and identify. After the Japanese attack on Pearl Harbor on December 7, 1941, America would remain at war through the next four Christmases. Sixteen million Americans would serve in the military and be stationed from the Philippines to North Africa to Fairbanks, Alaska. Even after the war, many military personnel remained stationed in Europe and Japan. American popular culture highlighted these Christmas separations in a variety of ways. "During World War II newspapers exhibited pictures of soldiers, taken during the holidays," writes James H. Barnett in *The American Christmas,* "and displayed marked sympathy for those unable to return home for Christmas."[10]

In a single-page piece in *Life* in 1941, a soldier has been photographed with his girlfriend. His arm is around her waist, and their faces are close to one another's as they say goodbye. The article notes of the young man's farewell: "And what he dreamed of principally was his Christmas furlough. . . . But now with the nation at war, most Christmas furloughs will be drastically cut or cancelled altogether, and this farewell scene takes on a deeper significance."[11] Soldiers wishing to return home played a significant role in the popularity of songs like "White Christmas," "I'll Be Home for Christmas," and "Have Yourself a Merry Little Christmas." These songs reached soldiers by Armed Forces Radio, USO shows, and jukeboxes.[12] For many soldiers, these new, nostalgic Christmas songs captured and poignantly expressed the feeling of separation from home, friends, and family. "Christmas meant home, warmth, security, and a sense of roots; war was the antithesis of all of that."[13]

The war mobilization would also cause mass population displacement on the home front, as millions of Americans aided the war effort as factory workers, nurses, and volunteers. Many women would enter the workforce for the first time, leading to a significant rise in the number of married women who worked.[14] African Americans also migrated to both the North and the West during World War II, and by 1944, two million blacks worked in war plants.[15] Cultural historian Philip H. Ennis underlines the significance of these migrations in *The Seventh Stream*. "The movement of people was unquestionably the most pervasive and important fact of the war years. It was the greatest mass migration the country had ever seen. Over fifteen million civilians crossed county lines in pursuit of jobs or family. The crowding, the scarcities, the uncertainty, and, above all, the disruption of the familiar placed a heavy burden on the expressive culture the migrants brought with them or found in strange locales."[16]

But America's nostalgic mood had deeper roots than World War II. Standing on the precipice of a new era that would be bolstered by economic prosperity at home and political influence abroad, many Americans felt anxious. Rapid change in the twentieth century had seemingly divorced Americans from familiar traditions and staid rituals. "To those old enough to remember it, the America of 1896 returned in quaint images," writes Lloyd Morris in *Postscript to Yesterday*. "In fifty years it had become almost as remote, very nearly as idyllic, as the America of the founding fathers."[17] "White Christmas," "Have Yourself a Merry Little Christmas," and "The Christmas Song" expressed a desire to turn back the clock on the modern era, to cling to a way of life that had vanished.

The broader changes in American lifestyles were highlighted by changes in transportation, communication, and living spaces. In *Postscript to Yesterday*, Morris compares 1896 to 1946, noting the changes that left many Americans uneasy. While perhaps diminished in economic importance in 1896, rural and small town America still existed. Even Americans who grew up in the city still had roots in the countryside. Everyone traveled by carriage, boat, or train; there were no super highways and no automobiles to drive on super highways. Even after the invention of the telephone in 1876, most distant communication by everyday Americans took place by U.S. mail; while a few houses may have had electric lights, very few were wired for a more extensive use of electricity. Also, there were no wars in foreign lands in 1896 requiring Americans to travel far from home (the Spanish-American War would begin in April of 1898). "Who would have anticipated more than momentary interest in pictures that flickered, or horseless locomotion?" Morris notes. "And certainly there seemed to be little possibility that men would fly until they became angels."[18] In 1946, Americans lived in cities and increasingly, thanks to the automobile, moved to suburban houses wired for modern kitchen appliances, radio, and telephones. By 1946, any connection with an idyllic nineteenth-century America had been severed. Marty Jezer notes in *The Dark Ages*, "The postwar years nailed the coffin shut on the American past."[19]

But Morris was interested in more than the technological changes that altered the face of the American landscape. The disappearance of older ways of living meant more than a change in America's physical landscape or the reality of the phonograph, air travel, and vaccinations. The older ways had also been supported by mores and customs, guidelines for social behavior and etiquette, and an intricate value system. All were woven together into a more or less agreed upon social contract between millions of Americans. Morris notes this shift and the resulting collective American identity crisis:

> Culture asserted that all mechanisms exist to serve spiritual ends; that so far as they fail to do so, they are being misused. The social order, the economic structure, and even the state are instrumental devices; their object is to produce a wider freedom and more universal welfare in which men may achieve the good life. And the good life is that which completely fulfills the spirit. Why, culture asked, had Americans been betrayed into identifying means with ends? Why had they so complacently sacrificed the needs of the spirit to the uses of purely material progress? Why had they rejected the life of values for the life of mere things? Why had they harnessed their superb transforming instruments to the dollar, instead of to the liberation and enrichment of existence?[20]

One could argue that despite the anxiety underlying rapid change, Americans ultimately embraced the automobile, electricity, and talking pictures; and that Americans embraced the abundance of the expanding consumer culture with little hesitation. But beneath the physical facts of modern change lay a deeper spiritual disruption, a fear that an important component of American life had been irrevocably lost.

The nostalgia of "White Christmas" and other melancholy holiday songs tapped into the American psyche and the general feeling of disconnection from the past during the early to mid-1940s. It was a mindset that placed a new emphasis on memories and the past, a past that seemed more and more divorced from the world that Americans inhabited. "White Christmas" and "Have Yourself a Merry Little Christmas" favored a pre-twentieth-century or at least a premodern America filled with small towns, villages, and farms—rural settings stripped of cars, electricity, radio, and war. These ballads searched for a simpler time and place devoid of the perceived complexities and spiritual void of modern life. More than a white Christmas, Americans were dreaming of escape from the hustle and bustle of Christmas present.

Nostalgia occupied a significant place in the thoughts of Americans during the 1940s, and it was a mood that assured that songs tinged with memories of yesteryear like "White Christmas," "Have Yourself a Merry Little Christmas," and "The Christmas Song" would receive a warm welcome from American listeners. It is ironic, then, that it was a new mass media—part of the cultural upheaval that had fueled Americans' anxious mood—that brought these songs to an American audience. "The new, aggressively nostalgic Christmas entertainment," notes Jody Rosen in *White Christmas,* "embodied a central paradox of commercial Christmas culture: they were modern, big-city, mass-media products that sold the holiday as a retreat from, and rebuke to, high-tech urban modernity—a trick that seems the essence of city-slicker salesmanship."[21] Through the local movie theatre, the diner jukebox, and the radio in the family living room, Americans, en masse, indulged in the same mood. "For centuries revelers sang solemn carols," writes author Susan Waggoner. "Then something exciting happened. Electricity. The radio. Movies. A booming record industry. It was an explosion of sound, usually mushrooming around the ears of holiday shoppers."[22]

The technology that had created vacuum tubes and film projectors and the manufacturing culture that made radios and phonographs affordable were wrapped up in the same forces that had changed the American landscape from agrarian to urban and replaced the family dairy farm with the textile factory. A 1941 ad for a Sparton automatic radio-phonograph promised:

> **A Remarkable Buy** for Christmas! This compact 5-tube, 110 volt AC superheterodyne Sparton table model, radio-phonograph does everything but think—and saves you plenty of money besides! Automatically plays and changes 12 ten-inch or 10 twelve-inch records, brings you standard broadcast and American-Foreign short wave. Equivalent to 8-tube operation. Cover closes down when in operation eliminating surface noise. Complete with 6-inch electro-dynamic speaker, built-in loop antennae, tone control and permanent type needle. Handsome walnut veneer cabinet with contrasting African walnut trim. Be sure to put this marvelous Sparton model on *your* Christmas list.[23]

The new technologically savvy recording industry also recognized the importance of Christmas to sales. Tongue in cheek, *Billboard* noted in 1943 that record retailers expected "old Kris to

FIGURE 2.2. "For Christmas! Give This Treasure-trove of Entertainment," 1956 advertisement. John W. Hartman Center for Sales, Advertising & Marketing History.

deliver about 25 per cent of their yearly business"[24] American consumers may have decried the hustle and bustle of Christmas in the mid-1940s, but every time they bought a copy of "White Christmas" they were lending support to a trend that had undercut the song's idyllic vision of an old-fashioned holiday in the backwoods of rural America.

Nostalgic Songs for a Nostalgic Era

> I still can't listen to "I'll Be Home for Christmas" or Bing Crosby's record of "White Christmas," or Judy Garland in *Meet Me in St. Louis* singing "Have Yourself a Merry Little Christmas" . . . without getting a lump in my throat.
>
> Richard R. Lingeman, *Don't You Know There's a War On?*

IF AMERICANS wished to turn away from the bustle of Christmas present during the 1940s to reminisce, songwriters, singers, and the music industry were more than glad to feed this indulgence. The success of the industry in the production and marketing of Christmas music had little to do with innovation: the industry had already honed effective ways of delivering music to a popular audience by radio and 78-rpm records. The trick had been in discovering a new niche market that could be explored and exploited in popular song, one that simply allowed songsmiths to draw from and build onto a long tradition of winter and Christmas imagery.

It is difficult to imagine contemporary Christmas music without "White Christmas," "Have Yourself a Merry Little Christmas," and "The Christmas Song." Each has attained classic status alongside sacred carols like "Silent Night," "Away in a Manger," and "The First Noel." But while the sacred songs borrow from familiar Christian mythology surrounding the holiday, these songs from the 1940s provided a mythology carved out of the American soil. By celebrating fir trees, falling snow, and other seasonal clichés, these songs have been woven into the fabric of an American Christmas and have become part of the national consciousness.

All three of these songs are unhurried ballads that create an open setting for quiet reflection. The intimate tone of each song is conversational, a soulful prayer overheard, a personal letter, or

FIGURE 2.3. Currier and Ives, "Winter Morning in the Country," ca. 1873. Print: lithograph, hand-colored. Library of Congress.

a late-night, long-distance phone call from someone dear. The quiet tone personalizes the delivery of each lyric, and it is easy to imagine the singer addressing a friend, a spouse, a child, or even the listener. Each of these songs offers an invitation to the listener to stop for two or three minutes and enter a quiet reverie with the singer. Each song's hushed mood seems to cue the listener: *it's okay to relax, there's no hurry.*

These songs, in essence, created a mental space that seemed to exist outside a modern Christmas. For the duration of each song, the listener dreams with the singer, and the hustle and bustle of modern Christmas fades into the distance; each time a jukebox spun "White Christmas" and "Have Yourself a Merry Little Christmas," you could forget about shopping, Santa, and the ongoing war; each time Bing Crosby or Judy Garland or the King Cole Trio sang these songs in a movie or for holiday radio specials, you could escape into a dream of the perfect American Christmas.

By drawing from familiar imagery and setting a reflective mood, each of these songs gives the illusion of having captured the spiritual impulse at the heart of an American Christmas. Together these songs offer a wistful vision of yesteryear, one celebrated with family and friends and rooted in the rural landscape and values of a preindustrial America.

"White Christmas" (1942)

> The song's images of sleigh rides and falling snow and eager children capture the mythic essence of the American Christmas.
>
> Jody Rosen, *White Christmas*

WE HAVE become so familiar with "White Christmas" that it is easy to overlook many of the song's details. We barely notice, for instance, the short instrumental passage that opens the song, or the light orchestra that offers a tasteful backdrop to Bing Crosby's reassuring voice. Likewise, the choir that repeats the lyric in the second half of the song easily fades into the background. The elements that support the emotional current of the song, that leave a residue of comfort and solitude, are taken for granted. Even the warmth of Crosby's voice, gently stretching phrases, bending syllables, and, at one point, whistling, are no more or less than we expect. Over a time span of nearly seventy years, "White Christmas" has simply become a familiar and accepted cornerstone of the modern Christmas holiday in America.

All of these overly familiar elements, however, work in unison to create the affecting import of "White Christmas." The song's pace, for instance, is unhurried, helping to set the mood for Irving Berlin's lyric and Crosby's vocal. Even as the arrangement of singer, backing vocals, and orchestra swells in volume, the combined musical sound remains a simple hush. The leisurely tempo and quietude become even more evident as "White Christmas" comes to a close. At this point, the already unhurried pace is brought to a standstill, setting the stage for Crosby to deliver the last line. As he begins, all of the instrumental backing and choir drop out, leaving a silent calm that the listener might associate with falling snow. Crosby's finale, eventually reunited with the choir and bells, extends for twenty seconds. From the opening instrumental passage to Crosby's finish, each of these elements serves to instill an expressive mood into "White Christmas."

This reflective frame of mind carries over into the emotional resonance of the lyric. As "White Christmas" begins, Berlin's narrator seems to be daydreaming, imagining Christmases from an earlier time in his life, carrying on an inner dialog. This inner dialog is clearly a memory play, perhaps tinted by imagination; it expresses the thoughts of someone far from home (physically, mentally, or spiritually), and longing for return and reconciliation. But while the images he recalls may lack specific details, they do draw a realistic sketch of a certain kind of place. He dreams of glistening treetops, sleigh bells, Christmas cards, and, most of all, snow. These images are grounded in rural America and perhaps even an earlier America, one similar to the winter engravings of Currier and Ives and the winter paintings of Grandma Moses. Moses, remembering her childhood in an earlier America, writes in her autobiography:

> After dinner we all went over to the Whiteside Church where the Reverend Henry Gordon gave a lovely talk on Thanksgiving. The church was warmed by wood fires, and the pulpit was trimmed with evergreens and oak bows with acorns on them, quite pretty.
>
> Mr. Abbott took us home from church, we had our first sleigh ride for that year. It was lovely, tucked into the sleigh with buffalo robes, bells a' jingling, and then to enter our home so warm and cozy, with coal fires, surely we should have been thankful, and I think we were.[25]

A person would have to live near treetops, after all, to see them glistening, and one would have to own horses—not cars—to hear sleigh bells. Even taking the time to write Christmas cards evokes a leisurely pace not associated with the busyness of the modern holiday season. At the end of the song, the narrator breaks his solitary reverie to offer a direct holiday salutation to the listener: a sincere wish that the listener will find the same holiday cheer that he seeks.

There is a hymn-like quality to "White Christmas," which may seem strange for a song that is seemingly secular in content. The quietude and simplicity of the lyric, arrangement, and performance has a peaceful, restful air, and it would be easy to hear the narrator's inner dialog as a spiritual meditation. The unifying symbol is the whiteness of the snow, an image of purity that blankets and brightens the bare trees and straw-colored fields during

FIGURE 2.4. *Holiday Inn,* 1942. Bing Crosby and Marjorie Reynolds. By permission of Paramount Pictures/Photofest.

winter. The narrator believes that a white Christmas will have the power to make the world anew, or more accurately, to return it to an earlier, more perfect state.

It is also easy to see these ideas and the theme of nostalgia working themselves out in other popular culture artifacts from the era, including the movie that helped introduce "White Christmas," *Holiday Inn* (1942).

In *Holiday Inn,* Crosby's character Jim Hardy opens an inn to celebrate a number of American holidays, an idea bathed in patriotism reflective of the national mood relating to World War II. In a quieter moment in the film, Crosby introduces "White Christmas" in the company of his future love interest, Linda Mason (Marjorie Reynolds). It would be inaccurate to describe the setting of this scene as a typical American home; the fireplace and mantel are much too large. But the room does present a homey atmosphere. Crosby, dressed in a casual robe and smoking a pipe, and his inn, ensconced in rural Connecticut, offer a picture of harmony and tranquility; the contemporary performance world that he left behind, where song and dance acts perform on Christmas Eve in Manhattan, has disappeared. In this pastoral setting, Crosby introduces "White Christmas," and in this version of the song, he's joined by Reynolds (with the vocal sung by Martha Mears). Warmed by the wood fire, the scene and setting offer a comfy vision of rural American life in winter.

This vision seems far away from the setting of the original and seldom recorded opening verse for "White Christmas." Initially, a brief introduction placed the song's narrator in Beverly Hills as Christmas approached, basking in the sunshine but yearning to be up North. Berlin believed that the images of a warm Hollywood diminished the appeal of "White Christmas" and eventually removed the opening verse from the sheet music. Crosby never sang this section. There was little nostalgia to be found in sunny L.A. and little possibility that oranges and palm trees would offer a comfy vision of a rural American Christmas.

"White Christmas" was not the first Christmas song to indulge in romance with the American past, but never had a song joined so many Americans together in a similar mood. It was embraced by American soldiers away from home, dreaming of their own white Christmases, and embraced by their loved ones at home, dreaming of a speedy reunion with the soldiers. Berlin's spare lyric gave Americans an attractive though bare-bones medium that allowed all listeners to fill in their own memories. In this way, the lyrics of "White Christmas" were tinged by fondly remembered childhoods, recollections of friends and loved ones, and reminiscences of happy days gone by. In essence, "White Christmas" helped usher in a new era for the Christmas song, offering all Americans a chance to indulge in the sacred hush of yesterday.

"Have Yourself a Merry Little Christmas" (1944)

Have yourself a merry little Christmas
It may be your last
Next year we may all be living in New York
Hugh Martin/Ralph Blane

WHILE MANY listeners may remember that Judy Garland sang "Have Yourself a Merry Little Christmas" in *Meet Me in St. Louis* (1944), they may nonetheless find it difficult to travel back to her original, darker version of the song. It is likely, for instance, that they are more familiar with Frank Sinatra's version from 1957, and equally likely that listeners associate the song with the same pleasant, lingering nostalgia of "White Christmas." After all, whether listeners consider Sinatra or Garland's version, or note the slight difference between the lyrics of each version, the result should be more or less the same: both singers, after all, are wishing a special someone "Merry Christmas."

Without considering the deeper resonance of Garland's vocal, there is little on the surface to suggest that her version of "Have

Yourself a Merry Little Christmas" was somehow darker. The song's narrator is simply asking an unnamed person to forget all of her troubles during the holiday season. The first two verses of "Have Yourself a Merry Little Christmas" carry this same basic sentiment, with the narrator bidding her listener to enjoy Christmas, disregard current difficulties, and believe that by the following year, everything will be better. While the song's bridge may be less comforting, its glance back to happier days seems like little more than nostalgic reverie. As the third verse brings "Have Yourself a Merry Little Christmas" to a close, the reference to the fates and muddling through until life gets better suggests little more than quaint clichés from an earlier era: life may not always turn out as we wish, but if we persevere, it will always get better. As the last line repeats the song's title, the melancholy of the lyric has been swept away like yesterday's cobwebs.

It has been noted that Ralph Blane and Hugh Martin's original draft of "Have Yourself a Merry Little Christmas" for *Meet Me in St. Louis* had been much darker, and, by implication, that the rewritten version sung by Garland in the movie was somehow less gloomy.[26] The original draft suggested that the current Christmas celebrated in the film may be the Smith family's last or at least the last Christmas that the family would spend in St. Louis; not surprisingly, a number of people involved with the movie found the lyrics depressing. Eventually, Martin agreed to rewrite the song, replacing the gloomy lyrics. It would be easy, reading about and noting the changes, and noting the emphasis placed on the removal of the offending passages, to guess that the final version that Garland sang for *Meet Me in St. Louis* was a happier one that captured the American Christmas spirit.

FIGURE 2.5. *Meet Me in St. Louis,* 1944. Judy Garland and Margaret O'Brien. By permission of MGM/Photofest.

But this quick reading of "Have Yourself a Merry Little Christmas" remains too close to the lyric's surface, too removed from the inflections of Garland's rendition of the lyric. As Garland sings the opening lines of "Have Yourself a Merry Little Christmas," the strings provide a tasteful cushion beneath her deeply expressive vocal. Her voice is full and emotive, adding pulsating vibrato, increasing depth of volume during the bridge, and, as the song comes to a close, drawing out her words. The emotional pull of Garland's voice is also self-absorbed within the lyric, leaving the impression that she has fallen deep into reverie, that she is singing to herself more than anyone else. Her mood, withdrawn and disheartened, tints the lyric a melancholy blue. As the orchestra slackens its already languid pacing, Garland unhurriedly utters the final line of the song, adding even more feeling to her Christmas wish.

Even with the altered lyric, there remains an unsatisfied yearning in "Have Yourself a Merry Little Christmas," a yearning for the warm glow of yesteryear; the yearning is so strong that it threatens to transform a harmless melancholy for the past into a deeply felt expression of sorrow for what cannot be regained. The measured tempo itself seems to inject a downhearted element into the lyric's wish for a merry Christmas, a mood that is enhanced and solidified by the melodic sweep of the song's bridge. And while the lyric itself may be saying "merry Christmas," Garland/the song's narrator is trying too hard to convince her listener and perhaps herself that there will be a merry Christmas. The dreamy references to "golden," "yore," and "faithful friends," along with the need to muddle through what—to many—should be the happiest time of year, leaves the listener caught in a downward spiral of holiday blues.

Garland's reading of "Have Yourself a Merry Little Christmas" catches and expands the anxious undercurrent of Martin and Blane's lyric. Even as she offers her heartfelt Christmas wish, she never believes it; even while she may deliver her wish with sincerity, she seems unable to rise to the sentiment. A persistent irony undercuts the lyric each step of the way, leaving the listener with a much darker holiday lullaby than later versions of the song might suggest.

When listening to the lyric of "Have Yourself a Merry Little Christmas," it's easy to recall *Meet Me in St. Louis,* the movie in which the song appeared in 1944. For the span of the movie, the viewer would never guess that St. Louis was anything but a pleasant town where the upper middle class built multistory dwellings to house their large, happy families. The Smith family, mom (Mrs. Anna Smith), dad (Mr. Alonzo Smith), grandfather (Grandpa), five children (Esther, Tootie, Rose, Agnes, and Lon), and housekeeper (Katie), lives in what appears to be a spacious, old-money home. The father of the clan is employed as a banker, an apparently comfortable job that allows him to amply support his family: the family eats well, everyone dresses immaculately, and they can afford hired help. *Meet Me in St. Louis* is a Technicolor version of family life in small town America, circa 1900.

This perfect way of life, however, is threatened when the father is offered a job in New York City. Within the movie, St. Louis is imbued with the warmth of tradition and sense of graceful permanence; New York is a modern and anonymous city. While it might seem a stretch to consider the Smiths' crisis as tragic, the viewer, for the duration of the movie, is invited to do so.

This crisis reaches its pinnacle at Christmastime. In the midst of the winter sequence of the movie, Garland's Esther Smith sings

"Have Yourself a Merry Little Christmas" to her troubled sister Tootie (Margaret O'Brien), attempting to comfort her by recalling perfectly imagined days from the past and wishing for their return. Colloquially speaking, Esther seems to be trying too hard to put a positive spin on the Smith family's current problems. Tootie, however, remains as unconvinced as Esther, and tears well up in her eyes as she listens. Following the song, Tootie runs outside, picks up a stick, and violently dismantles a snow-person family in the backyard. Her reasoning is simple: if the snow family cannot accompany the Smiths when they move to New York, then no other family that inhabits the house should be allowed to have them. "Have Yourself a Merry Little Christmas" finds the Smith family at its nadir, and Garland's version of the song permeates the lyric with these qualities, generating a residue that overflows from the movie.

While "White Christmas" concocts a dreamy quality of an affectionately remembered American holiday, "Have Yourself a Merry Little Christmas" evokes a sadder mood. The quaint references to "yuletide" and "yore" in "Have Yourself a Merry Little Christmas" mine a barely recalled American past, while references to troubles and the fates delve into the less hopeful side of holiday nostalgia. One can always hope to be reconciled with friends and family, but these reconciliations cannot be guaranteed; one can dream of the return of golden days, but fate may have other plans in store. In the place of hope and happy dreams, one waits, muddling through troubled times. Instead of optimism for the future, a favorite American quality, "Have Yourself a Merry Little Christmas" expresses the belief that the best of what life has to offer has been buried in the past. Enamored of distant memories, "Have

Yourself a Merry Little Christmas" offers a backward glance at a misty golden era anchored in an earlier America.

"The Christmas Song (Merry Christmas to You)" (1946)

> "The Christmas Song" is suffused in the same fuzzily reminiscent glow—best expressed in its subtitle, "Chestnuts Roasting on an Open Fire"—as "White Christmas," and its impact was just as immediate.
>
> Dave Marsh and Steve Propes, *Merry Christmas, Baby*

IT MIGHT BE easy to think of specific Christmas songs as alluding to particular American settings or to a particular time and place in the American past. In "White Christmas," for instance, a listener might imagine the Connecticut countryside of *Holiday Inn* or the Vermont of *White Christmas* (1954). Even if the setting is less specific, certain places—perhaps climates known for their warmth and sunshine, like Florida and California, or climates known for harsher winters, like Alaska—are definitely ruled out. Likewise, "Have Yourself a Merry Little Christmas" may evoke a specific place, like the St. Louis of *Meet Me in St. Louis,* or simply recall an older, nineteenth-century America with its use of yuletide, olden days, and yore.

Locating "The Christmas Song" in a specific time and place proves a more difficult task. While "The Christmas Song" does present a winter setting, there is no snow; and while roasting chestnuts may seem like an old-fashioned pastime, the song never lets on that this is an activity—in the mid-1940s, following the chestnut blight—relegated to Christmases of yesterday. Perhaps even the brazen act of naming it "*The* Christmas Song" adds a universal touch that moves the song from a specific time and place.

In a sense, "The Christmas Song" borrows from these earlier songs, consolidates all they offer, and moves beyond them by presenting an expansive vision of an American Christmas. Instead of providing images of snow or a golden yesterday, "The Christmas Song" presents a smorgasbord of symbols—chestnuts roasting, turkey, mistletoe, Jack Frost, and choirs singing carols—and serves as a brief sketch of the perfectly realized American Christmas. The quiet reverie of the earlier songs based in nostalgia, with each narrator's persona intimately addressing the individual listener, has been set aside; regional images of a New England winter or the distant rural past have likewise been discarded. Instead, Nat Cole's narrator addresses a larger set of listeners, perhaps a set of friends gathered to roast chestnuts or sing carols, and offers them a more up-to-date version of an American Christmas. Nostalgia for an American Christmas anchored to the past remains, but Cole's version of "The Christmas Song" has one foot in the modern era.

Much of this mood is conveyed in the tone of the King Cole Trio's arrangement of "The Christmas Song." In a short space, the intricacy of the strings, guitar, and bass create a sophisticated blend of light jazz that places the listener at ease. Cole's silky vocal style adds the final element. His mild delivery clearly relies on an amplified microphone, a quality that places him within the crooner tradition. Cole's style, however, has smoothed out the dips and swoops of a crooner like Crosby, and he never attempts to carry the pathos of Garland. Instead, he has compressed his voice to the warmth of his natural speaking tone. These smoother

FIGURE 2.6. "A Chestnut Vender, Baltimore, Md," (between 1900 and 1906). Glass negative, 7 × 5. Detroit Publishing Company Photograph Collection; Library of Congress.

qualities work well with the more optimistic lyric; the nostalgia of Cole's persona might be described as quiet reminiscing.

This warmth imbues the lyrics of "The Christmas Song" with a pleasant glow, though Cole's even tone also compacts the emotional depth of the lyric. Blending with the guitar, bass, piano, and strings, his vocal tone, tenor, and delivery are perfectly in sync with the song's arrangement. Compared to the simplicity of the earlier songs discussed, "The Christmas Song" seems quite intricate, urbane, and modern.

While the arrangement helps to set the mood, at least one element of the lyric updates the song for modern America. Near the end of the second verse, the listener is told that children will find it difficult to sleep at Christmas, because Santa Claus will soon arrive. Children naturally anticipate the toys that Santa has loaded on his sleigh and will likewise be curious to discover whether reindeer can fly. By adding children and Santa Claus, "The Christmas Song" removes a great deal of the melancholy associated with earlier nostalgia-trimmed songs.

Despite the modern sensibility and milder nostalgic vision of "The Christmas Song," its leading symbol—the chestnut—tints the song with a wistful vision of a bygone time and place. In *American Scientist,* David Vandermast writes:

> The chestnut can be considered an iconic American tree for many reasons, not the least of which is the reference to chestnuts roasting on an open fire in "The Christmas Song," by Mel Tormé and Bob Wells. Ironically, the song was written in 1944, just as the last wild American chestnuts were succumbing to the blight. By 1946, at the peak of the song's popularity,

it would have been hard to find any American chestnuts to roast.[27]

Even by 1946, then, the American chestnut had nearly disappeared from the tapestry of holiday traditions.

The great American chestnut forest, primarily located in the Appalachians, had been a rich source of timber, tannin, and chestnuts at the beginning of the twentieth century. While business owners and local entrepreneurs profited from the chestnut, many families relied on the yearly chestnut harvest to provide needed food and clothing supplies before the winter. When the chestnut burr opened and released its fruit in the fall, families would gather the harvest and trade with local store owners, who shipped chestnuts by train to urban centers like Baltimore. The chestnut represented an essential element of rural life as it was experienced in the Appalachians at the turn of the twentieth century.[28]

By the time of the release of "The Christmas Song" in 1946, the eastern forest of American chestnut had mostly been decimated by an imported blight first discovered at the Bronx Zoo in 1904. The blight moved quickly from north to south, destroying the fruit-bearing trees and continuing to destroy any new chestnut growth before the tree reached maturity. Even before the demise of the chestnut, traditional Appalachian culture, seemingly one of the last American rural outposts, had been modernized by highways, electricity, and telephones. The chestnuts that "The Christmas Song" pictured roasting on an open fire belonged to an older way of life, now no more than a memory.

But Cole's reading of the lyric never dwells on or expresses concern over what became of the American chestnut. Instead, the final

instrumental notes of "The Christmas Song" offer nothing more than a pleasantly wistful reference to another beloved holiday song from the latter half of the nineteenth century, "Jingle Bells."

In the brief nostalgic coda of "The Christmas Song," Oscar Moore's guitar becomes more audible, breaking in as Cole finishes the last syllable of the song. The listener may even remember the guitar from the opening of the song, or perhaps from a brief solo in the middle. Moore's coda temporarily picks up the pace, allowing his chorded solo of "Jingle Bells" to stand out clearly. "The Christmas Song" dovetails nicely with these notes, paying homage to an American classic.

While Moore's coda may add a slightly wistful air to the song's ending, "The Christmas Song"—as a whole—is clearly moving in a more cheerful direction. Less haunted by the past, the lyric only embraces pleasurable images and memories from America's Christmas heritage. Yes, Christmas may be represented by many symbols grounded in the past, but we can also look forward to Santa, presents, and excited children; to roasting chestnuts, feasting on turkey, singing carols, and kissing beneath the mistletoe. It is a sense of nostalgia a listener might find in a winter-themed Hallmark card.

In a sense, the more upbeat mood of "The Christmas Song" seems to mirror the American public's post–World War II mood: the soldiers have come home, the economy is booming, and the future is brimming with possibilities. Expressing little concern over America's discontinuity with the past, "The Christmas Song" has smoothed the kinks out of holiday melancholy, turning the tide toward a more hopeful vision of an American Christmas in which the past is no more than pleasant memories. With "The Christmas Song," nostalgia has become memory without pain.

A Nationalized Christmas

> The inspiration of great music can help to instill a fervor for the spiritual values of our way of life; and thus to strengthen democracy against [its enemies].
>
> Franklin D. Roosevelt

> The only bad feature of my life in the Army is missing Christmas at home. Although Christmas morning doesn't mean so much as it used to I can still appreciate the Christmas season. I hope and pray that this will be the last Christmas so many boys will be away from home, in an Army camp, at Christmas. That's why we're here now, so that in years to come folks can enjoy their own way of living.
>
> C. C. Witherow

As Americans went to war at the end of 1941, it would have been easy to imagine that celebrating Christmas—when compared to life and death on the front line—might seem frivolous. Even the materials needed to make Christmas records and movies—shellac for records and celluloid for film—would deprive the fighting men and women of the U.S. military of valuable resources. While the U.S. government required numerous sacrifices on the home front during the war, the celebration of Christmas—like baseball and the movies—was deemed an American right and duty. As with popular culture in general, celebrating Christmas—modestly decorating one's home, sending care packages overseas, and maintaining family ties at home—was much more than mere entertainment: these holiday rituals had the power to distract, build morale, and reinforce a broader belief system. "The celebration of the American Christmas—that magically sanctified and

ostentatiously irreligious holiday—became a kind of patriotic act," writes Jody Rosen in *White Christmas*.[29]

While "White Christmas" and "Have Yourself a Merry Little Christmas" never mention the war, they—in evoking American values—"tapped soldiers' homesickness as well as domestic longings for a mythical past."[30] Originally, notes LeRoy Ashby in *Amusement for All*, the Office of War Information had encouraged Tin Pan Alley to write overtly patriotic songs and complained when too few were forthcoming. In truth, however, very few of these songs caught on, mostly because Americans (including soldiers away from home) preferred "sentimental tunes about home, families, and girl- and boyfriends—not rip-roaring marching music."[31] "White Christmas" fit that description. Karal Ann Marling notes:

> With its wrenching evocations of home and loved ones and snow and yesterday, "White Christmas" explained what Americans were fighting for in Europe and the Pacific—and later, Korea—as they sent their requests to hear Crosby's record on Armed Forces Radio. . . . More than just a Christmas song, it spoke in simple, direct language of the state of quasi-religious grace that the American Christmas had always aimed to attain: an ideal combination of nature and culture, trees and cards, memory and anticipation, innocence, and the dream of home.[32]

Inversely, then, "White Christmas" and other nostalgic songs were patriotic in evoking an American way of life—the promise of family and home but also of democracy and egalitarianism.

FIGURE 2.7. Franklin D. Roosevelt, Hyde Park, New York, 1943. Franklin D. Roosevelt Presidential Library and Museum.

The same modern media that allowed "White Christmas," "I'll Be Home for Christmas," and "Have Yourself a Merry Little Christmas" to reach millions also allowed the president to gauge and guide the American mood during the war years. Early in 1941, Franklin D. Roosevelt's Four Freedoms speech outlined the rights pertaining to everyone throughout the world: freedom of speech and worship along with freedom from want and fear. During the National Christmas Tree Lighting ceremony of 1941, Roosevelt reinforced these democratic principles by emphasizing the centrality of Christmas in the life of a nation:

> Our strongest weapon in this war is that conviction of the dignity and brotherhood of man which Christmas Day signifies—more than any other day or any other symbol.
>
> Against enemies who preach the principles of hate and practice them, we set our faith in human love and in God's care for us and all men everywhere.
>
> It is in that spirit, and with particular thoughtfulness of those, our sons and brothers, who serve in our armed forces on land and sea, near and far—those who serve for us and endure for us—that we light our Christmas candles now across the continent from one coast to the other on this Christmas Eve.[33]

As Rosen notes, "Christmas had long been the de facto national holiday, but now President Roosevelt made it explicit."[34] The vision of a Christmas homecoming blended with the righteousness of the American cause; the vision of war blended with a vision of home and family.

While national nostalgia would come and go depending on America's good fortunes, a backward glance to olden times and forgotten ways remained a perennial for the Christmas celebration. As Marsh and Propes write, "In 1945, World War II ended but not the seasonal nostalgia it had unleashed."[35] Likewise, holiday songs and seasonal nostalgia remained encoded with a broader set of American beliefs and values: Christmas, especially between the early 1940s and early 1960s, remained one with the national cause. During World War II, when Americans longed for the stability of home, family, and tradition, holiday songs reflected that desire. Speaking of the reception of "White Christmas," Irving Berlin

said, "The boys in the South Pacific must have read into ['White Christmas'] cranberry sauce, roast turkey, Christmas carols, the family around the hearthside, a glowing Christmas tree."[36] Christmas songs were American Christmas songs.

FIGURE 3.1. “Seeing Santa Claus,” 1876. Print: wood engraving. Library of Congress.

3

Santa Claus: A Bag Full of Toys

There
is abundant
evidence that Santa Claus
is enormously important to
the American Christmas and has
become the central figure of the folk
celebration, comparable in importance
to the Christ Child in the Nativity.

James H. Barnett, *The American Christmas*

Merchants
may readily
appropriate Santa Claus for
use in advertising because he
is . . . [the] god of *materialism* and
is thus a highly appropriate seasonal
model to portray with products that
represent the good things in life.

Russell W. Belk

You
can keep Christ out
of Christmas but not Santa.

James B. Twitchell, *Adcult USA*

If "White Christmas" (1942) spoke to homesick GIs and Americans yearning for an earlier place and time, songs like Gene Autry's "Here Comes Santa Claus" (1947) more clearly defined the postwar zeitgeist. Americans continued to listen to nostalgia-tinged songs during the latter half of the 1940s and throughout the 1950s, but increasingly these songs stood at odds with the pulse and pace of Christmas present. Middle-class Americans may have dreamed of snow-covered lanes, Grandmother's house in rural Pennsylvania, and roasting chestnuts on an open fireplace, but they increasingly lived in cities and suburbs, drove Packards and Fords on state highways (and soon federal highways), and worked in middle management at Mutual of Omaha, GM, and DuPont. And whether listening to the adult-themed "I'll Be Home for Christmas" or the child-themed "Rudolph the Red-Nosed Reindeer," they most often heard these songs on Western Electric radios and RCA record players, not from church choirs or neighborhood carolers.

The American economic recovery began slowly. As the economy grew out of the decade-long Depression during the war (1941–1945), the need for military provisions—uniforms, Spam, jeeps, tents, Coca-Cola, and tires—made it difficult for manufacturers to keep pace with consumer demand. Many consumer goods, including bicycles, rubber shoes, and typewriters, were rationed. Once manufacturers began to refocus on consumer goods at the end of 1945, returning soldiers and families on the home front were ready to splurge. Viewed as the starting point to a new consumers' republic, the postwar years are described by Lizabeth Cohen: "As each family refurbished its hearth after a decade and a half of depression and war, the expanded consumer demand

12/14/45

This Year He's Coming Home for Christmas

During December a total of over a million men are expected to arrive in this country from overseas. Their first thoughts will be of getting home as fast as a train can carry them there — home for Christmas for the first time in several years.

Their urgent travel needs will require a considerable portion of the space on our trains and those of other railroads over the Holidays. Extra equipment is not yet available, as so many Pullman cars and coaches are still employed in moving this military personnel from ports of arrival to separation centers.

So in thinking of travel this Holiday season, consider the boys who may have spent last Christmas in a fox hole, prison camp, or at sea, and to whom coming home this Christmas means so much.

FLORIDA EAST COAST Railway

A Florida Industry and Institution

FIGURE 3.2. "This Year He's Coming Home for Christmas," 1945. Advertisement. John W. Hartman Center for Sales, Advertising & Marketing History. By permission of Florida East Coast Railway, L.L.C.

would stoke the fires of production, creating new jobs and, in turn, new markets."[1] Post–World War II growth was phenomenal by any standard, and the central economic fear in 1945–46—that the American economy would sink back into another depression—remained no more than a phantom. "The period of affluence that began in 1946," writes historian Marty Jezer, "would last more than two decades."[2]

For Americans steeped in habits of frugality and the value of saving, the change from famine to feast also needed a new moral framework. Near the end of *It's a Wonderful Life* (1946), George Bailey (Jimmy Stewart) is shown what Bedford Falls would have looked like if he had never been born. Bedford Falls is now Pottersville, named after the money-grubbing banker Henry S. Potter (Lionel Barrymore). The quaint small town has been transformed into a freewheeling small city filled with vice and ugliness; it is a nightmare vision of human virtue turned inside-out by a hyper focus on the bottom line. "In place of community George finds feckless mobs bent on brutal sensation and numbing pleasure," writes historian Charles F. McGovern. "He confronts a world whose inhabitants have lost their souls and their ability to love. All they have is a relentless grind of getting and spending: misery-making work in a suffocating prison of cheap stores, billboards, saloons, and dance halls, all awash in a ghastly neon glare."[3] Pottersville is director Frank Capra's vision of capitalism run amuck.

But Capra's vision of small town life and the dangers of consumer society failed to move most Americans in 1946. They may have felt the pangs of nostalgia as small town America faded into the rearview mirror, but the suburbs, filled with new homes, and the department stores, stocked with an abundance of easily available goods, beckoned. As McGovern notes in *Sold American*, Americans preferred the vision of *Miracle on 34th Street*, with a grandfatherly Santa Claus serving as the kinder face of commerce. When *Miracle*'s Kris Kringle selflessly sends Macy's customers to other department stores, he proves that businesses can help the consumer and ultimately, by earning his or her loyalty, make more money. The New York City of *Miracle on 34th Street* may lack the local charm of Bedford Falls, but it never leaves the impression of an immoral wasteland like Pottersville. Far from corrupt and nightmarish, the urban landscape is dotted with clean, well-lit department stores and pleasantly attired clerks and salespersons.

Capra seeks to convince the viewer that the American system requires the guiding hand of government and good men like George Bailey to operate smoothly in *It's a Wonderful Life*; director George Seaton argues that the system has no serious flaws and can pretty much take care of itself in *Miracle on 34th Street*. Leaving the thrift of the Depression behind, Americans wanted to believe they could prosper as consumers and remain virtuous at the same time. Whether *Miracle* and "Here Comes Santa Claus" spoke the people's mind or just repeated what the people wished to believe about themselves, these popular culture products offered a philosophical underpinning for the postwar American mindset.

The virtue of the new American consumer was bolstered by a creed set forth by political leaders and the business community following the war. As sacrifice and the purchase of war bonds had defined patriotism during World War II, consuming would define love of country following the war. "Utilizing the expanded capacity for consumer goods was not mere self-indulgence but had become vital for the economic health of the nation," writes historian William B. Waits. "Political leaders as well as others believed that high government spending during the war had produced full employment, thereby ending the Great Depression. With the advent of peace, they became deeply apprehensive that consumption would drop precipitously, dragging the economy back into an economic morass. Consumption of production was, to them, a national priority."[4]

On the most basic level, consumption would fuel the economy, creating greater demand for products, a growth in the manufacturing and service industries, and the expansion of the job market. All of this, in turn, would create more products to buy and more consumers to buy them. Consumption—buying a new house or car, starting a family, and even splurging at Christmas—would guarantee that no economic slump or slowdown would occur. "The new postwar order of mass consumption deemed that the good purchaser devoted to 'more, newer and better' was the good citizen."[5]

As was true long before December 1945 (the first Christmas following World War II), the Christmas shopping bump had been a recognized phenomenon. Many consumer items—jewelry, liquor, clothing, and records—sold in larger quantities in December than any other month. In *The American Christmas,* James H. Barnett documents the December bump during 1950. Averaged per month, sales in any category would have equaled 8.3 percent. In December 1950, however, retailers greatly exceeded this average, achieving 14.8 percent in department store sales, 16 percent in men's clothing and furnishings, and 22.7 percent in jewelry.[6] For stores selling items positively impacted by the bump, achieving Christmas sales became the most crucial retail event of the year.

Expanding even beyond the usual sales bump, the post–World War II economic boost was remarkable. "During the first three Christmases following the war—1945, 1946, and 1947—seasonal sales were strong, reflecting the continuation of wartime prosperity into peacetime," notes Waits. "The volume of sales increased about 10 percent per year, to the delight of retailers who stood to gain a lot."[7] While these levels could not be sustained, they nonetheless revealed an American public attempting to make up for lost time.

During the Christmas seasons after the war, middle-class Americans decked out their suburban homes with holiday decorations and purchased a cornucopia of nonnecessities from Woolworth's, JC Penney, and Montgomery Ward. While this version of the American Dream failed to spread to all Americans, postwar prosperity seemed an economic miracle that would eventually—given time—bless everyone. "Reconversion after World War II raised the hopes of Americans of many political persuasions and social statuses that a more prosperous and equitable American society would finally be possible in the mid-twentieth century due to the enormous, and war-proven, capacities of mass production and mass consumption," notes Cohen. "The new growth economy of the Consumers' Republic promised more affluence to a greater number of Americans than ever before."[8] The more one bought, the more one bolstered the democracy of the American market. And no time of year provided a better reason to display and indulge in this prosperity, or to express one's patriotism, than Christmas. As Americans settled into an era of prosperity defined by conspicuous consumption, Santa Claus and Rudolph offered consumer-friendly symbols that buried the machinations of the holiday market under happy urban folktales.

Santa Claus: The Kinder Face for Christmas Commerce

> Although Coca-Cola did not invent Father Christmas/Santa Claus, it can claim to have finally fixed his identity.
>
> John Storey

SANTA CLAUS had been an important fixture of the American scene before the mid- to late 1940s, though his image, habits, and companions had been altered over time by illustrators and ad men. Clement C. Moore had laid the foundations for an Americanized Santa Claus in "A Visit from St. Nicolas" in 1823, establishing many of the elf's familiar habits (flying reindeer, a jolly disposition, and a sack full of gifts). Illustrator Thomas Nast offered an attractive visual equivalent during the 1860, and added a few more details to the story (a home at the North Pole, a workshop, elves, and a list for naughty and nice children).[9] As a modern American Christmas developed between 1880 and 1940, Santa proved an incredibly adaptable image and idea. Since Santa brought the gifts, he provided parents with an excuse to splurge on children.[10] "Santa, in effect, disguised the indulgence of parents from children and to some extent from the parents themselves," observes historian Gary S. Cross. "It was Santa, after all, not the parents, who heaped box upon box under the tree."[11]

During the 1920s and 1930s, advertisers helped fill in the fine details of Santa's persona while simultaneously utilizing his child-friendly image to reach the youngest set of consumers. Coca-Cola launched the premiere Santa ad campaign in 1931, cementing his appearance as far as the American public was concerned. "This new Santa quickly became everyone's impression of who and what

Santa Claus should be," noted Pam Stephenson.[12] Santa, with a bottle of Coca-Cola nearby, would gently coax children to buy the right soft drink. "Coca-Cola bottlers had always known that they had to snare the next generation of drinkers early, regardless of the taboo on direct advertising to those below twelve," writes historian Mark Pendergrast. "One approach directed at children wound up reshaping American folk culture through the art of Haddon Sundblom."[13] As Santa expanded his role as salesman for Coca-Cola, invading the home with calendars and cardboard cutouts, the space between his benevolent exterior and commercial underpinning became more difficult to separate.

The primary era for Sundblom's Coke Santa fell between the 1930s and the mid-1950s, a space in time when commercial illustration faced less competition from photography and television. Illustrations worked well for mass circulated magazines like *Life* and *Saturday Evening Post,* and Coke advertisements, early on, stood out simply because they were in color. *Life* may have filled its pages with photographs during the 1930s, but they were usually black and white photographs. Illustrators like Sundblom took advantage of their medium by creating vibrant images that dazzled the viewer. Perhaps they had seen Santa hundreds of times in advertisements, but never had the reds of his suit appeared so deep or the white trim of his fur lining so plush. "Disliking the cheap costumes and meager look common to department-store and charity Santas," note Barbara Fahs Charles and Robert Staples in *Dream of Santa,* "Sundblom countered with abundance—a lavish use of fur and leather (belt, boots, and gloves were all massive), a billowing beard, and a waistline so ample it required a belt and suspenders."[14] Whether seeing a Coke Santa writ large on a highway billboard or happening upon one while flipping through the pages of *National Geographic,* consumers small and large would have found the paintings difficult to miss.

Borrowing from both Moore's poetic vision and Nash's illustrations of St. Nicholas, Sundblom presented a cheery, heavy-set Santa, adorned in plush furs and painted in rich colors. "Sundblom's Santa was the perfect Coca-Cola man—bigger than life, bright red, eternally jolly, and caught in whimsical situations involving a well-known soft drink as his reward for a hard night's work of toy delivery."[15] To reach children, the indirect approach worked best: build an association between Santa, the patron saint of children, and Coca-Cola. Yes, there was ad copy that made the hard sell, but the image of Santa may have said more. While Santa never told the viewer to "buy a Coke," the repeated appearance of a bottle of Coca-Cola within the advertisements—in Santa's hand, in the family refrigerator, and left out as a gift on Christmas Eve—drew an easy association between St. Nick's favorite colors and those of the soft drink. If the advertisements were successful, it would eventually seem like a crime *not* to stock up on Santa's favorite cola for the holidays and *not* to leave a cold Coke out for Santa on Christmas Eve.

In the pages of *National Geographic, Boy's Life, American Girl,* and *Reader's Digest,* Sundblom's Santa Claus frequently engages the viewer with a direct gaze, reminding the magazine reader of Moore's elf: "A wink of his eye and a twist of his head / Soon gave me to know I had nothing to dread."[16] It is the direct gaze of the honest Yankee peddler, embodying the ethic of hard work and deserving, because of his labor, a break from time to time. In Coca-Cola ads, in fact, Santa is usually taking a break. In a 1935 advertisement, Santa takes a seat on a chair or small bench before a family's

Christmas tree, wiping the sweat from his brow; in 1936, Santa can be seen pausing during his busy night to play with a train set and doll; and in 1937, he helps himself to a turkey leg and a cold Coke from a refrigerator. In a 1958 advertisement, Santa is pictured relaxing in an easy chair with a reindeer curled up beneath it; in 1959, he is caught raiding the family icebox by a bright-eyed young boy; and in 1964, he "seems to have become a member of the family," sitting with a small girl on his knee and a small boy playing before them.[17]

As sentiment, Sundblom's vision of Santa's "whimsical" world, filled with toys and children and saturated in deep reds and plush whites, offered a mise-en-scène of an idealized American Christmas. It was a vision of the good life, filled with material abundance and a bright future. If the refrigerator that Santa raided in 1937 remained a luxury item to most Americans during the Depression, it was a luxury item that Americans could dream of and work and save for. Likewise, hard-working Americans could fill these refrigerators with fat turkeys and plenty of Coca-Cola. Especially after the war, Americans would also fulfill the dream of starting a family with happy, healthy children who naturally loved Santa and never forgot to leave him a Coke. It would be a world where Santa delivered the goods, regardless of whether a child had been naughty or nice. As Charles and Staples note of a 1951 Coca-Cola ad with Santa resting at a table beside a giant book filled with children's names, the pages are titled "Good Boys and Girls."[18] The naughty list has disappeared. Sundblom's paintings created more than a connection between Coca-Cola and Santa Claus: he created a connection between Coke, Santa, and an idealized vision of the American way of life.

Because Sundblom's Coke Santas have been exhibited like art, it is easy to forget that all of these images would have been seen in public spaces as advertisements between 1931 and 1964. When a family entered a grocery store, they were greeted with a 54-inch Sundblom Santa, offering them a cardboard Coca-Cola; when driving down the highway, larger-than-life Santas, pasted onto billboards, promised that "Thirst asks nothing more"; and in the home, Santa arrived on Coca-Cola calendars and dozens of other products offered or given away by the company.[19] First and foremost, these advertisements and promotional items were designed to sell Coca-Cola products. Whatever appeared in Sundblom's Coke Santa illustrations between 1931 and 1964, one item was always front and center: a bottle or bottles of Coca-Cola. Sometimes stopping for the "pause that refreshes" after a hard evening's work or raiding a family's refrigerator, Santa gently pushed the fizzy brown cola on all Americans.

As the post–World War II era unleashed a consumers' republic, Santa Claus became the kinder face of commerce for the all-important holiday shopping season. Santa may have represented the joy of the season and the love of children, but there was no easy way to separate him from the market. The use of Santa as salesman, toy promoter, and general goodwill ambassador was in sync with modern America during the latter half of the 1940s and throughout the 1950s. These connections also brought the world of commerce closer to the world of childhood. Sundblom's dream of Santa was that of an affluent America, where the economic pie continued to grow larger and everyone got a bigger slice. Santa with his bottomless sack of gifts became inseparable from the American Dream, promising each child abundance and material gain without limits.

The Mythic and Modern Santa Claus

While new Santa songs would be issued between 1934 and 1945, the market seemed primed for Christmas music and Santa songs—old and new—after 1945. While noting exceptions, Tim Hollis writes, "The big explosion of Christmas songs—especially those aimed at kids—did not take place until the period of postwar prosperity and the glut of new children it produced."[20] Santa songs, first and foremost, were songs about and for children.

Two of the earliest Santa songs, "Jolly Old Saint Nicholas" and "Up on the House Top," provided a number of musical and lyrical flourishes that later Santa songs would draw from. It remains uncertain when either song was written or who wrote them; it does appear that both followed in the footsteps of Moore's "A Visit from St. Nicholas" and were perhaps written in the latter half of the nineteenth century. Because much of Santa mythology has remained constant, these songs have never seemed out of place amid more contemporary material.

Paying close attention to the lyrics of "Up on the House Top," the listener learns a number of facts about Santa. The modern listener, child or adult, takes most of these facts for granted. Traveling back to the time of the Civil War (1861–1865), however, many children may have been unaware of these basic myths. We learn from "Up on the House Top" that:

1. Santa has flying reindeer.
2. He is referred to as both Santa Claus and St. Nick.
3. Santa enters each house by sliding down the chimney.
4. Santa brings toys to the little ones (children).

In "Jolly Old Saint Nicolas" we also learn that:

1. Santa Claus comes on Christmas Eve.
2. Santa carries a pack of toys on his back.
3. Children ask Santa for toys.

While both songs covered a handful of familiar myths, one item sticks out: toys. Both songs focus heavily on the toys that children wish for and that Santa will bring.

Because most of the folklore detailed in "Up on the House Top" and "Jolly Old Saint Nicholas" appeared to be derived from sources such as "A Visit from St. Nicholas," they helped promote familiar myths. The Santa songs that followed in 1932 ("Santa Claus Is Comin' to Town"), 1947 ("Here Comes Santa Claus"), and beyond were grafted onto these familiar molds and, like the Coca-Cola ads, filled in a few popular folklore details. Unlike the earlier songs, these new songs would be disseminated much more widely by records—spinning at 78, 45, and 33⅓ rpms—as well as on radio broadcasts, restaurant jukeboxes, and home phonograph players. Unlike earlier folk cultures that unfolded in regional pockets, records were distributed and promoted by large companies like Columbia and RCA throughout the United States and abroad. Even while there were frequently multiple recordings made by different performers of any given song, everyone had access to the same versions of these recordings. Songs like "Santa Claus Is Comin' to Town" and "Here Comes Santa Claus" may have borrowed heavily from past myths, but they now served to circulate a modern vision of Santa to millions of children.

As a group, Santa songs featured a number of motifs that separated them from nostalgic fare like "White Christmas" and "I'll Be Home for Christmas." Nostalgia may have played a role in

FIGURE 3.3. Thomas Nast, "Caught!," ca. 1892. Print: wood engraving. Library of Congress.

these songs (indeed, nostalgia seems to play a role in everything associated with an American Christmas) but was not a prominent feature. While there will be more to say about these motifs when considering individual songs, it might be helpful to consider a brief outline of these ideas.

1. Santa Claus Mythology. Santa songs often borrowed and repeated familiar Santa myths: he travels by sleigh, he has flying reindeer, he carries a bottomless toy sack, and he slides down chimneys. Many of these details are drawn from Moore and Nast's Santa and serve both as a familiar reference and to establish Santa's character and vocation. Part of the fun of Santa songs is recognizing the familiar folklore.

2. Present Bringer. Whatever Santa's various features, one stands out: the main purpose of his visit, when all is said and done, is to bring toys to boys and girls. In this role, his generosity holds no bounds, thanks to his bottomless magic sack. Santa songs may choose different details to sketch his character, but without the toys and the anticipation of toys, the other details fall flat.

3. Kid Centered Songs. Most Santa songs are about children and primarily for children. They are happy songs, upbeat and bright, about the joy of Christmas and the excitement of anticipating Santa's arrival. Even seemingly negative messages (the need to be good as a prerequisite to receiving presents) are pasted over with jaunty sleigh bells and bright trumpets: the modern Santa remains omniscient, but he no longer punishes. Within the realm of the Santa song, Christmas is focused on and primarily for children.

4. Adaptability to the Modern Era. While Santa has a number of traditional traits in song, he is adaptable to the modern era. Instead of a sleigh he can rely on a helicopter or a train; while steeped in European legends, he can also learn the latest trends, like dancing the boogie-woogie. In one Coca-Cola cardboard cutout from 1957, Santa is pictured in a rocket, and in one Gene Autry song, he arrives in a whirlybird. With Santa, modernity holds no

threat to tradition. While up to date on the latest toys and modes of travel, Santa nonetheless retains his familiar appearance and performs his customary tasks.

5. A Saint, Embodying American Values. While Santa has often been considered a secular figure, he continued to retain spiritual abilities. His magical powers allow him to bring presents to all the children of the world in one night. Santa, between Moore, Nast, and Sundblom, also came to embody broad American values. Like a good small "d" democrat, he never makes a distinction between rich and poor, and he supports the American way of life by offering the hope of material goods to all children. Combining these spiritual and homegrown values, Santa Claus becomes, in Russell Belk's words, "the god of *materialism*," celebrating the American creed of material progress for all.[21]

6. Christmas Materialism Decontaminated. Even though Santa is the god of American materialism, the issue of money is never directly broached. Because Santa songs are child centered, they can expound the joys of getting lots of gifts while side-stepping the issue of money. The innocence of the child is matched with the magical nature of Santa: children want shiny toys, and Santa has the ability to make them appear out of thin air. In this way, Santa songs seem to stand outside consumer culture even while singing its praises. Belk writes, "Thus, even though Santa is the god of materialism, he retains his sacredness by giving only pure gifts."[22]

In 1945 and 1947, respectively, two Santa songs would reach large audiences: Bing Crosby and the Andrews Sisters' version of "Santa Claus Is Comin' to Town" and Gene Autry's "Here Comes Santa Claus." "Santa Claus Is Comin' to Town" had been written in 1932 by Fred Coots and Haven Gillespie, though the first version by Harry Reser and His Band was only recorded in 1934. Autry wrote "Here Comes Santa Claus" with Oakley Haldeman, borrowing the happy phrase that children shouted during the Santa Claus Lane Parade in Los Angeles in 1946. "Santa Claus Is Comin' to Town" was included on Crosby's *Merry Christmas* in 1945, an album that peaked at number one on *Billboard's* album chart every year between 1945 and 1950, while "Here Comes Santa Claus" peaked at number nine on *Billboard*'s pop chart two days after Christmas in 1947 and continued to appear on several other charts through 1950. These two songs and the Santa Claus myth would be supplemented in 1949 by an even bigger hit, "Rudolph the Red-Nosed Reindeer."

"Santa Claus Is Comin' to Town" (1932)

There is an intriguing opening section to "Santa Claus Is Comin' to Town" that would have originally been referred to as the verse, a lead-in section that sets up the song. Verses seem to be fairly unusual in modern Christmas songs ("I'll Be Home for Christmas" also has an opening verse), and even when present, singers usually leave them off. The same opening sections were commonly used in classic songs by Cole Porter and Irving Berlin (Berlin lopped off his own opening verse to "White Christmas"). "The verse has always been an orphan," notes William Zinsser in *Easy to Remember*, "sung in the original Broadway show or Hollywood musical and then abandoned on the commercial record."[23]

In the verse to "Santa Claus Is Comin' to Town," the song's narrator explains that while taking a trip to the Milky Way, he decided to stopover at the North Pole for a vacation. "I just came back from a trip along the Milky Way / I stopped off at the North Pole to spend the holiday / I called on old dear Santa Claus to see what I could see."[24] In this fashion, the narrator learns about Santa's forthcoming holiday visit.

This playful opening, though seldom heard, sets the mood for the remainder of the song: "Santa Claus Is Comin' to Town" has all the attributes of a children's song. Adults may also appreciate it, but the song's subject—Santa's arrival—and its easy rhyming meter leave the impression of a nursery rhyme set to music. As a children's song, "Santa Claus Is Comin' to Town" does not intend to educate children about Christmas rituals or offer instructions

FIGURE 3.4. *Miracle on 34th Street,* 1947. Edmund Gwenn and Natalie Wood. By permission of 20th Century-Fox/Photofest.

on the moral underpinning of receiving gifts. The song primarily offers familiar information, Christmas myths known to most American children of the time. Its overall purpose—musically and lyrically—is to celebrate the arrival of Santa. Even though "Santa Claus Is Comin' to Town" is frequently sung and has been made popular by adult singers, performing the song too seriously or at too sluggish a pace seems to work against its intent. If Santa Claus was the patron saint of children, then Santa songs were happy hymns of praise for the presents he brought to boys and girls, good or bad.[25]

Understanding the opening verse and comprehending "Santa Claus Is Comin' to Town" as a playful children's song helps explain the most seemingly incongruous section of the lyric. Looking back from today, it may seem rather odd that the most prominent lyric in the song issues a threat: if children do not watch out and if they are bad and cry, they might miss out on Santa's Christmas visit. Children are also reminded or warned that Santa Claus can see them all the time, even when they are sleeping; he has the ability to weigh whether a child has been good or bad. Today, it would be easy to imagine that gifts were withheld from children during the 1930s and 1940s when "Santa Claus Is Comin' to Town" first became popular.

Within the song, Santa Claus has the same omniscience as the Christian deity. Like the Christian God, he has the power to punish those who fall short morally, though his power, unlike God's, is limited to withholding Christmas presents (or replacing them with switches). Presumably a bad child can also—through a heartfelt effort—become a good child, receiving forgiveness from Santa. If he or she does not receive presents this year, then surely Santa will bring gifts the following one.

The oddity of the lyric, however, is the emptiness of the threat, both within the broader American culture and within the song itself: the American Santa Claus always delivers. The idea of a companion like Black Pete who accompanies Santa and delivers a bundle of sticks or lumps of coal lost favor in nineteenth-century America: middle-class parents wanted to shower gifts on children, not punish them. And when merchants attached Santa mythology to parades, store promotions, and product advertisements, there was little incentive to suggest negative outcomes. As Gary S. Cross observes, "There is no sale in punishment."[26] While well-worn folklore insists that Santa Claus kept a list of naughty boys and girls, the threat failed to convince. Even children, while perhaps enjoying the recognition of a well-known strand of the Santa legend, no longer believed the threats. Folklorist Alan Dundes notes, "Santa Claus gives gifts to children whether they are good or bad, threats to the contrary notwithstanding. The child expects to be rewarded, magically, whether he deserves it or not."[27]

The emptiness of the warning in "Santa Claus Is Comin' to Town" is also undercut by the music itself. Like many other Santa songs, Coots's music is upbeat and jaunty, embracing the joy and fun of Christmas anticipation. The song is likewise free of minor chords, even on the bridge that emphasizes the warning that children should be good. In Crosby and the Andrews Sisters' version, cheerful horns lay a path for a popularly hip recording of the song. Crosby's vocal asides and lightheartedness undercut any bite that the lyric might have, while his vocal interplay with the Andrews Sisters concocts an easy swinging feel: even without the opening verse, the child-friendly intent of the song is clear. Carefree and easy flowing, this version of "Santa Claus Is Comin' to Town" leaves the impression that Crosby, taking a break from the nostalgia of "White Christmas" and solemnity of "Silent Night," had offered one for the kids.

Why reserve so much lyrical space for a threat that is never meant to be taken seriously? For fun, perhaps. In addition to the happy music, the lyrics are made up of very simple myths that have been passed down by adults and the broader American culture about Santa Claus. The child, listening to the song, enjoys recognizing the familiar Santa stories. There is also fun in the easy, light rhymes—"twice" with "nice" and "awake" with "goodness sake." This is a happy song, meant to mimic the excitement of Santa's forthcoming visit to children and the pile of presents wrapped in shiny paper. While omniscience and the threat of punishment would remain qualities featured in Santa songs, the balance between Santa as moral watchman and Santa as gift bringer would be definitively tipped toward the latter.

The remainder of the lyric emphasizes the real message of "Santa Claus Is Comin' to Town": the bonanza of toys that he will bring on Christmas Day. There will be horns, drums, an elephant (though one might wonder what a child would do with an elephant), and dolls, among other items, enough to build a toy town around the Christmas tree. The bounty, made up of a copious number of toys that served no practical purpose save to entertain children, was the material end of Santa's visit. The shopping store windows, letters to Santa, and the restless sleep on Christmas Eve all climaxed in Santa delivering the goods.

Curiously, from a narrative point of view, "Santa Claus Is Comin' to Town" (as well as "Here Comes Santa Claus") placed the greatest emphasis on the anticipation of Santa's arrival—even more than on the presents themselves. While the song certainly highlights presents, it expresses little concern with Christmas morning and the unwrapping of those presents. By Christmas morning, after all, Santa has already come and gone. As Dundes writes, "The real excitement of Christmas is the anticipation of Christmas eve or day. The present is always a little disappointing in comparison with the high hopes for the future."[28] Instead of Christmas Day, "Santa Claus Is Comin' to Town" builds excitement by focusing on the immediacy of Santa's visit. Whether he is coming to town, as in "Santa Claus Is Comin' to Town," or down Santa Claus Lane, as in "Here Comes Santa Claus," it seems as though he may arrive at any moment. As nostalgic songs like "Have Yourself a Merry Little Christmas" projected back to a golden yesteryear, songs like "Santa Claus Is Comin' to Town" projected forward to the possibilities of tomorrow.

"Here Comes Santa Claus" (1947)

Gene Autry often repeated the story that he got the idea for "Here Comes Santa Claus" while riding his horse Champion in the Santa Claus Lane Parade in Los Angeles in 1946. After Autry wrote the lyric, Oakley Haldeman set it to music. When Autry's version was released as a single in 1947, it reached the mainstream pop charts. While similar to Coots and Gillespie's approach in "Santa Claus Is Comin' to Town," Autry's lyric placed even more emphasis on Santa's arrival and the joy that he would bring. Likewise, Autry showed very little concern with the myth that naughty boys and girls would not receive presents. "Here Comes Santa Claus" is centered on one simple idea: a child's world at Christmas. The joy that children expressed during the Santa Claus Lane Parade was the same joy that all American children experience as Christmas Eve draws near. Autry's song, like "Santa Claus is Comin' to Town," is a children's song, celebrating the holiday from a kid's perspective. The sleigh bells mentioned within the lyric are transformed into real sleigh bells jingling in the song, suggesting that Santa—in the present tense—is on his way.

If "Here Comes Santa Claus" focuses more clearly on Santa's arrival than other myths, the song does present a number of ideas and instructions that may strike the contemporary listener as being as out of place as the threat of punishment in "Santa Claus Is Comin' to Town." While Santa has often been viewed as a secular figure, Autry easily combines Santa folklore with more traditional aspects of a sacred Christmas. The lyric repeats that children should say their prayers because Santa Claus is coming. While the reference is not unequivocally Christian—Jesus is never mentioned within the lyric—it is easy to gain that impression; children are also instructed within "Here Comes Santa Claus" to give thanks to the Lord above and that peace on earth can be achieved by following the light. While this commingling of sacred and secular symbols of Christmas may seem at odds, the sacred aspects serve only to underscore the arrival of Santa. Within "Here Comes Santa Claus," Santa's values and purpose—even when material based—easily blend with Christian ideals.

Also intriguing are Autry's allusions to class and endorsement of broad democratic principles in "Here Comes Santa Claus." Santa, the lyric notes, does not draw lines between the rich and poor. Furthermore, since everyone is a child of God, everyone is equal. Santa, like the Lord above of the lyric, makes no social or presumably any other distinctions. Autry's holiday philosophy endorses democratic Christian principles while also sanctioning the material bounty that Santa is bringing to *all* boys and girls. "Here Comes Santa Claus" offers the implicit understanding that Santa, if not an American himself, certainly endorses essential American ideals, values, and aspirations.

Folklorist Richard Dorson, writing about "Yuletide Gift-Givers," more explicitly identifies the modern Santa Claus as American:

> The Santa Claus figure is indeed a tubby caricature of Uncle Sam. He embodies the American love of well-being, the American dream of abundance, and the American spirit of democratic joyousness. Santa Claus visits *every* home in our United States, and he *always* leaves good things. The bright packages under the Christmas tree are the physical symbols of the land of plenty, and the tangible proofs of her rewards to the deserving. Young Americans see in the shiny miniature cars from the packages the sleek roadsters they will one day own. And their parents recognize in Santa the cheery angel who speaks for American productivity and salesmanship.[29]

Even if Autry's and other lyrical versions of the modern Santa Claus fail to spell out all of his American qualities, these qualities are easily understood. They have been woven into the fabric of the folklore related to Santa's role within American culture following World War II.

If Santa Claus—on the radio, at the movies, and pasted on billboards—had become a symbol of the American way of life to Americans by the end of the 1940s, he also served in the same role when exported to other cultures and nations. In 1949, two years after Gene Autry scored a hit with "Here Comes Santa Claus," he reprised the song in a B-Western called *The Cowboy and the Indians*. As the plot comes to a climax, Autry (playing himself) leads a caravan of charitable donations destined for the local Indian

FIGURE 3.5. Iwasaki Hikaru, "Granada Relocation Center, Amache, Colorado," 1943. Negative. National Archives.

reservation. After having written a report to Congress and prodded a small town reporter to write about the plight of local Native Americans, Autry has procured these goods as a gift "From America to the First Americans." We eventually learn that it really is Christmas (the Western setting does not immediately suggest a particular season), and Autry's ranch hand, Tom Garber (Hank Patterson), is dressed as a skinny Santa Claus. As Autry and the caravan reach the reservation, the school children join in, joyfully singing "Here Comes Santa Claus."

If there was any doubt that "Here Comes Santa Claus" was primarily intended for children, Autry and Columbia left one more clue: following in the footsteps of Coca-Cola, Columbia designed a colorfully illustrated record sleeve to catch the eye. On the sleeve of the single of "Here Comes Santa Claus," a jolly, cartoon Santa is waving to the viewer as he pops out of a stocking. Unlike the Coca-Cola Santa Claus, he is dressed in blue but is still easily recognizable thanks to his beard and traditional cap and by the fact that he is on the cover of "Here Comes Santa Claus." Dave Marsh and Steve Propes note in *Merry Christmas, Baby*:

> Another marketing innovation directly connected to Christmas records emerged in the late forties with Gene Autry's "Here Comes Santa Claus" and "Rudolph the Red-Nosed Reindeer." Those discs came with the earliest examples of the 45-rpm picture sleeve. This was little more than a sales technique based on the theory that if a youngster or his mother were shopping for records, and the kid spotted a colorful cartoon picture of Santa on the sleeve of "Here Comes Santa Claus," junior would pester mom until she put some cash into the pocket of the shrewd record marketer.[30]

The children's market, both for records and for merchandise in general, would become increasingly important as the baby boom grew into a generation of young consumers.

"Rudolph the Red-Nosed Reindeer" (1949)

In 1939, eight years after Sundblom had finished his first illustration of Santa for Coca-Cola and seven years after Coots and Gillespie had written "Santa Claus Is Comin' to Town," a new holiday story supplemented and expanded the familiar legends. Working for Montgomery Ward, Robert L. May created *Rudolph the Red-Nosed Reindeer* as an assignment: instead of buying coloring books to give away to children each year as it had in the past, the department store would create and distribute a product in-house. Montgomery Ward gave away at least 2.4 million copies of *Rudolph the Red-Nosed Reindeer* before World War II paper shortages brought production to a halt. After the war Montgomery Ward gave Rudolph's copyright to May, who proceeded to market Rudolph as a franchise, licensing a new version of the book, comic books, and multiple toys. The pace of the Rudolph franchise accelerated when Columbia Records issued singing cowboy Gene Autry's version of "Rudolph the Red-Nosed Reindeer" in 1949 (written by May's brother-in-law, Johnny Marks). If folk customs and commercial aims had shaped the Americanized Santa Claus over a hundred-year period, Rudolph was on an accelerated path: between 1939 and Autry's massive hit in 1949, Rudolph had become Santa's main sidekick and a superstar in his own right.

Anyone writing about how Rudolph reflected American values during the 1940s and beyond would have to start with James H. Barnett's (1954) and Alan Dundes's (1967) observations on May's modern folklore.[31] Much like the modern Santa Claus song, Rudolph's story is for children; more specifically, it is a children's story about overcoming adversity and earning, by personal effort, respect in the adult world. As a young deer (child) with a handicap that turns out to be an unrecognized asset, Rudolph comes to the rescue of an adult (Santa) at the last minute (on Christmas Eve). When Rudolph saves the day, he gains respect from both his peers (the reindeer who refused to include him in games) and the adult world. The story of Rudolph, then, is the fantasy story made to order for American children: each child has the need to express and receive approval for his or her individuality and/or special qualities. Rudolph's story embodies the American Dream for the child, written large because of the cultural significance of Christmas. Dundes writes, "It is the American child's success dream come true."[32]

FIGURE 3.6. Denver Gillen, "Rudolph the Red-Nosed Reindeer," ca. 1939. By permission of the Rauner Special Collections Library at Dartmouth.

As American individualism and entrepreneurship took center stage after World War II, it became clear that Rudolph's story had an element that was missing in the Americanized Santa Claus. While Santa Claus may occasionally take on a grandfatherly role, as in *Miracle on 34th Street* and within Sundblom's Coca-Cola illustrations, he remained a distant, unknowable figure, never detachable from his mythic qualities. Rudolph, however, is quite tangible as the reindeer next door who lends a helping hand to Santa. Selfless and full of pluck, Rudolph wishes for no more than to do the right thing. In May's *Rudolph the Red-Nosed Reindeer,* Santa asks Rudolph to guide his sleigh. Rudolph agrees, but stops to complete one last task before joining Santa and the other reindeer; even though Santa is obviously behind schedule, Rudolph, being a good reindeer, takes a moment to leave a note for his mom and dad. Whereas we can only know Santa generally, we know Rudolph as an individual; while we can only know Santa through familiar qualities, his suit, his sleigh, and his jolly laugh, we know Rudolph through his personal story of overcoming hardship.

In Johnny Marks's lyric and Gene Autry's version of "Rudolph the Red-Nosed Reindeer," May's story has been stripped to its bare essentials. We learn that Rudolph has a shiny nose and that he's been ostracized by the other reindeer because of his nose; when Santa asks Rudolph to use his glowing nose to guide his sleigh, however, he becomes very popular. The listener learns all of this information in just a little over the first minute of the three-minute song. Why do Marks and Autry give the entire story away so quickly and add almost no other details to flesh out Rudolph's famous ride? Perhaps because the story was already widely known. By the time Autry's version was released on Columbia Records in 1949, Montgomery Ward and May had already prepared the way with Rudolph books and merchandise. Marks and Autry needed no more than the bare bones of the story, a happy melody, and the addition of jingling sleigh bells and bright trumpets for a successful Christmas song.

For lasting value, Rudolph had one advantage over both previous and future supplemental myths to the Christmas story. Frosty the Snowman, for instance, was popularized in 1950 in another Gene Autry recording. Unlike Rudolph, however, Frosty seemed incidental to most familiar Christmas stories; unlike Rudolph, Frosty had few qualities that individualized his character. Rudolph, on the other hand, became the child-hero with American get-up-and-go within the familiar legend of Santa Claus. He added specific details to Santa's world, provided children with someone to root for, and reinforced the familiar Christmas folklore. Even as an individual, Rudolph had no interest in striking out on his own, creating countertraditions, or of overshadowing Santa. He simply wished to do his best to help Santa deliver presents so that all of the children would not be disappointed. If Santa is an American saint, then Rudolph is a self-effacing American hero.

Rudolph—as a protected trademark—also offered a commercial advantage that Santa lacked: while Santa remained in public domain, Rudolph could be tied to specific products, including songs and cartoons sold by specific manufacturers and producers. After Montgomery Ward returned the Rudolph copyright in 1946 or 1947, May developed his creation accordingly. One could buy a Rudolph lamp, a set of plates and mugs, a bib, a flashlight, and a snow globe. Rudolph's story was also converted into a View Master series. There was frequently a very fine line between the commercial and mythic Santa Claus, but he continued to appear in many noncommercial roles; no one owned the copyright, which meant the Salvation Army had as much right over Santa Claus's depiction as Coca-Cola. Rudolph, on the other hand, was brought to the public as a commercial promotion, a copyrighted idea that allowed May and others to control and exploit his market value. Perhaps because of this, very few Christmas songs featuring the famous deer followed "Rudolph the Red-Nosed Reindeer."

Rudolph also reflected the growing importance of the Christmas season to the national economy: in 1939, the year of Rudolph's birth, President Franklin Delano Roosevelt moved Thanksgiving to create a longer shopping season. FDR continued to play with the Thanksgiving date over the next two years (1940–41), though many states ignored his nonbinding proclamation. Despite opposition (Texas would refuse to change the date of Thanksgiving until 1956), it was easy to see that *if* Thanksgiving fell on the last day of November, it was bad for American retail. Eventually, Congress settled the matter, making the fourth Thursday (as opposed to the last Thursday) legally Thanksgiving in 1942. Christmas continued to focus on many intangibles—love of family, the home and homecoming, and a belief in Santa Claus—but these intangibles would be fueled by hard cash and underwritten by easy credit.

Christmas Commerce Following World War II

The release of *A Miracle on 34th Street* during the same year as "Here Comes Santa Claus" also denoted an intensified interest with Santa in song, movies, and radio. In *A Miracle on 34th Street*, an older man refers to himself as Kris Kringle (Edmund Gwenn) and believes that he really is Santa Claus. While his arrival in New York is not planned, it does seem to happen at the right moment: the modern world, filled with rational thought and greed, no longer understands the true meaning of Christmas. After being hired as Macy's Santa Claus by Doris Walker (Maureen O'Hara), Kris enters the life of Doris and her daughter Susan (Natalie Wood). While Doris likes Kris, she believes him deluded: she has raised Susan not to believe in fairy tales, which include Santa Claus. Because Doris and Susan's disbelief is representative of the worst side of modern rationality, they become a test case for Kris. By the movie's end, they are won over, convinced—as is the state of New York following a trial focused on Kris's identity—that Kris Kringle is really Santa Claus.

As in "Here Comes Santa Claus," *Miracle on 34th Street* offered an assumed rationalization of a modern Christmas based in consumption. While Autry's Santa makes no distinction between the rich and poor, *Miracle's* Santa embraces the broader material culture while censoring excess. While Autry's vision seems more class-based, derived from rural American values, *Miracle on 34th Street* remains more focused on the American Dream for the middle class in the suburbs. Although varying at important points, both views are reconcilable. Cobbled together, "Here Comes Santa Claus" and *Miracle on 34th Street* place faith in the American system to produce more stuff for more people; both offer an optimistic vision of a democratic economic system capable of raising all boats. We might think of it as "caring consumerism."[33]

While excess and greed remained, both "Here Comes Santa Claus" and *Miracle on 34th Street* make the argument that these are located in isolated pockets of the culture, that there is no reason to condemn the American way of life because of a few bad apples. At Christmas, more than any other time, businesses can learn to cooperate (as Gimbles and Macy's do in *Miracle*) and the haves can lend a helping hand to the have nots, rising above any shortcomings within the system. Santa's arrival was good news for every American child and anyone, anywhere who believed in American democratic values.

The logic of Santa and the postwar economy won over most American consumers. When business and political leaders promised endless expansion, Americans saw no reason to question whether that was possible. In its postwar incarnation, Christmas had become more than a fact of American life: receiving toys had become a perceived right and an economic necessity. Warning Judge Harper (Gene Lockhart) on the Kris Kringle case in *Miracle on 34th Street*, political advisor Charlie Halloran (William Frawley) notes that illogical or not, Judge Harper has no choice but to declare the older gentleman as Santa Claus:

> All right. You go back and tell them that the New York State Supreme Court rules there's no Santa Claus. It's all over the papers. The kids read it and they don't hang up their stockings. Now, what happens to all the toys that are supposed to be in those stockings? Nobody buys them. The toy manufacturers are gonna like that. So they have to lay off a lot of their employees, union employees. Now you got the C.I.O. and the A.F. of L. against you. And they're gonna adore you for it. And they're gonna say it with votes. Oh! And the department stores are gonna love you too. And the Christmas card makers and the candy companies. Oh, Henry, you're gonna be an awful popular fellow. And what about the Salvation Army? Why, they got a Santa Claus on every corner and they take in a fortune. But you go ahead, Henry. You do it your way. You go on back in there and tell 'em that you rule there's no Santa Claus. Go on. But if you do, remember this: You can count on getting just two votes, your own and that district attorney's out there.[34]

While these words may appear rather cynical on the page, the entire setting is focused on the humor of the situation. The implied rationality, however, underpinned the American understanding of Santa Claus and commerce from the end of World War II through the 1950s. Santa was good for business, children loved him, and the American economy was booming as never before. Questioning Santa Claus's value was foolhardy.

Even if a bystander had argued against the logic of Christmas present in America, these complaints would have more than likely fallen on deaf ears. Folklorists argued that Rudolph was fakelore, an industrial creation passed off as traditional folklore, but no one

FIGURE 3.7. *Miracle on 34th Street,* 1947. By permission of 20th Century Fox/Photofest.

seemed to care. Psychologists argued that parents used Santa to control children or promote consumption, but no one paid much attention. Many Americans may have worried that Santa was becoming more important than Jesus or that materialism was overwhelming the true meaning of Christmas, but in general, shopping remained an essential part of the modern holiday. In the bounty that seemed endless after World War II through the early 1970s, Americans were determined to celebrate Christmas in style, and no critic would rain on what promised to be an endless parade.

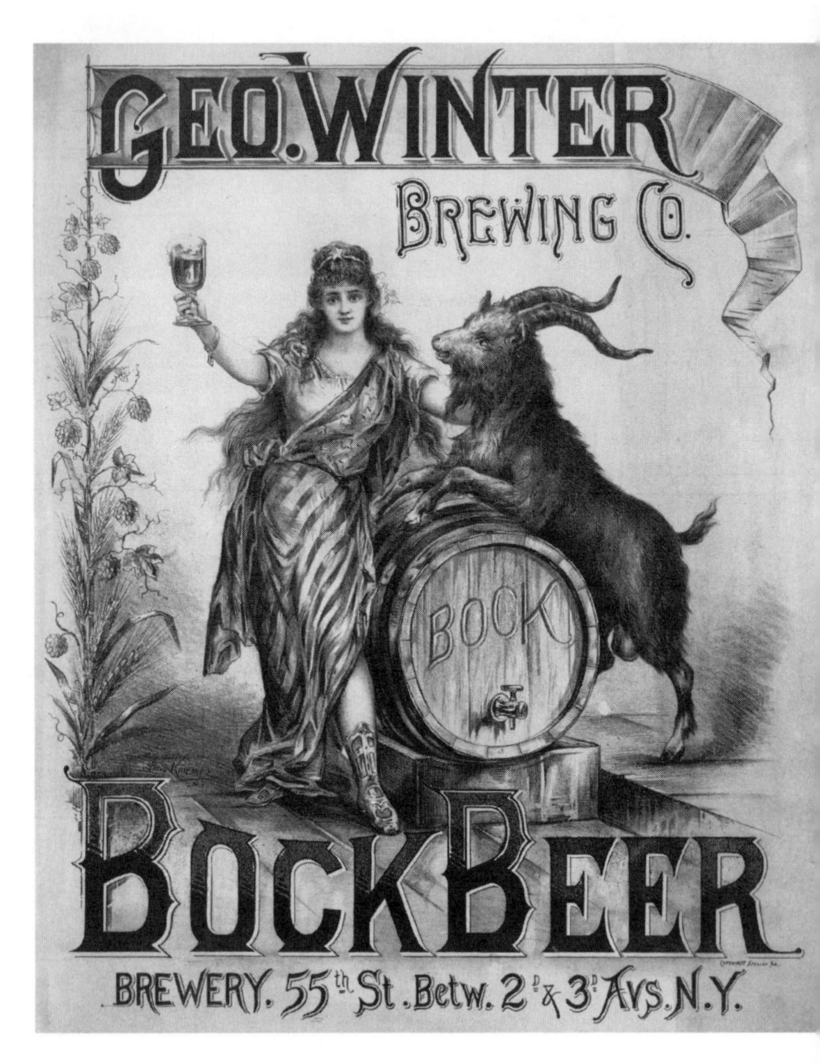

FIGURE 4.1. "Geo. Winter Brewing Co.," ca. 1900. Print: lithograph. Library of Congress.

4

Carnival: Beneath the Mistletoe

There were always people for whom Christmas was a time of pious devotion rather than carnival, but such people were always in the minority. It may not be going too far to say that Christmas has always been an extremely difficult holiday to *Christianize*.

Stephen Nissenbaum, *The Battle for Christmas*

Sex has always been as central as food to Carnival expressions of excess and enlargement.

Samuel Kinser, *Carnival, American Style*

Heaped up upon the floor, to form a kind of throne, were turkeys, geese, game, poultry, brawn, great joints of meat, sucking-pigs, long wreaths of sausages, mince-pies, plum-puddings, barrels of oysters, red-hot chestnuts, cherry-cheeked apples, juicy oranges, luscious pears, immense twelfth-cakes, and seething bowls of punch.

Charles Dickens, *A Christmas Carol*

In 1936–37, five to six years before Decca issued "White Christmas," Ben Light and his Surf Club Boys issued a novelty 78-rpm record titled "Christmas Balls." Light was known during that era for his party records, frequently featuring "blue" material with sexual overtones ("The Guy Who Put the Dix in Dixie"). The novelty of "Christmas Balls" was far from the novelty of children's songs like "I Saw Mommy Kissing Santa Claus" and "Nuttin' for Christmas," which reached *Billboard* charts during the 1940s and 1950s. "'Christmas Balls' burned with as many double entendres as your average pine tree has branches," write Dave Marsh and Steve Propes.[1]

"Christmas Balls" begins innocently enough with a jaunty piano playing "Jingle Bells," evoking holiday tradition and an upbeat mood. When the music shifts to an easy stride and the vocalist begins to sing (while "Christmas Balls" appeared under Light's name, it is unclear who sang the vocal), however, the vision of sleigh rides through the open countryside and Christmas innocence dissipates into a suggestive opening verse: "Christmas you know is not very far away / So I did all my shopping early today / I'm smiling 'cause I'm happy as can be / 'Cause I's a-gonna trim my baby's Christmas tree." Even as the listener catches on to the meaning, that trimming is a stand-in for sex, Light has barely gotten started on his Christmas sacrilege: "Let me hang my balls on your Christmas tree / I've got the nicest balls that you ever did see / No one else has balls like me / 'Cause I've seen many balls on the Christmas tree."

As a purveyor of blue records, Light and Hollywood Hot Shots (his label) seemed unconcerned that he might overextend his metaphor: humor—silly, rude, and obscene—remained the song's only guiding principle. Light seemed quite happy to mix and match metaphors on "Christmas Balls" until he had exhausted all puns and every possible double entendre.

Light's use of "balls" as a metaphor/pun ranges from sexual, hanging them on his girlfriend's Christmas tree, to points of danger: throughout the song, the singer's "Christmas balls" are in constant danger of snow, fire (from the lighted candles on the tree), and other obstacles. Outside of Light's outlandish invitation (to trim and hang his balls on his girlfriend's Christmas tree), he also admits to possessing a jealous streak: when Santa arrives, he will make him check his balls at the door before he fools around with his girlfriend's Christmas tree. By the song's end, Light's character is planning to go away on a trip, but he promises, like Santa, to return the following year to repeat the ritual.

FIGURE 4.2. L. M. Glackens, "Between Performances," 1907. Photomechanical print: offset, color. Library of Congress.

It is unclear whether Light's "Christmas Balls" was ever distributed very widely, though it certainly never received radio play in its own time. "Christmas Balls," however, was an early example of the carnival side of the holiday song, a style that drew from older carnival practices that rejected or simply ignored the Christmas tradition of home, children, and charity along with any religious connotations. From a Christian point of view, carnival practices (excessive food, drink, and sex) were immoral at best, pagan at worst; from a middle-class American point of view, these seemingly lower-class celebrations thumbed their noses at mainstream propriety.

While songs like "Christmas Balls" appeared as separate from sacred Christmas traditions, they had roots in multiple folk celebrations that dated before the birth of Christ. Festivals such as Saturnalia (Roman), Kalends (Roman), and Yule (German, English) were yearly celebrations of the harvest season. In many agricultural societies, the farmers and laborers had leisure time after the harvest to enjoy the fruits of the season. "Late-December festivals were deeply rooted in popular culture," notes historian Stephen Nissenbaum, "both in observance of the winter solstice and in celebration of the one brief period of leisure and plenty in the agriculture year."[2]

> It is difficult today to understand what this seasonal feasting was like. For most of the readers of this book [*The Battle for Christmas*], good food is available in sufficient quantity year-round. But early modern Europe was above all a world of scarcity. Few people ate much good food at all, and for everyone the availability of fresh food was seasonally determined. Late summer and early fall would have been the time

> of fresh vegetables, but December was the season—the only season—for fresh meat. Animals could not be slaughtered until the weather was cold enough to ensure that the meat would not go bad; and any meat saved for the rest of the year would have to be preserved (and rendered less palatable) by salting. December was also the month when the year's supply of beer or wine was ready to drink. And for farmers, too, this period marked the start of a season of leisure. Little wonder, then, that this was a time of celebratory excess.[3]

Besides food, drink, and leisure, multiple traditions like the Lord of Misrule (a mock king) and mumming (a costumed street party) temporarily turned the familiar social hierarchies upside down during festival season, calling for the highest to serve the lowest while heaping scorn on honored customs.

Whether these festivities offered an outlet for tensions between the rulers and the ruled, or whether they offered room for future social rebellion, remains an open question. The festivities offered at least a temporary rejection of the standing social order. On its most basic level, Peter Burke has noted, carnival was about having a good time. "Carnival was a holiday, a game, an end in itself, needing no explanation or justification. It was a time of ecstasy, or liberation."[4] While these traditions were often repressed by the church and state, they remained intertwined with folk life and culture. Even after the Catholic Church had established Jesus's birthday as December 25 in 336 A.D. (partly to curb festival excess, which usually occurred during the fall–winter harvest season), there was always a give and take between allowing and hindering festival rites. Even when repressed more harshly, carnival festivities continued to reemerge in both expected and unexpected ways.

In the early 1600s as Europeans began to settle America, these traditions traveled with them. While Christmas traditions varied widely in early American history (depending on region, the European origins of the inhabitants, and who controlled local government), they rarely focused on modern concepts of family and home, religion and consumption. Instead, Christmas and New Year's celebrations were often extroverted, public affairs that borrowed elements from older European festivals. Nissenbaum writes:

> Excess took many forms. Reveling could easily become rowdiness; lubricated by alcohol, making merry could edge into making trouble. Christmas was a season of "misrule," a time when ordinary behavioral restraints could be violated with impunity. It was part of what one historian has called "the world of carnival." . . . Christmas "misrule" meant that not only hunger but also anger and lust could be expressed in public.[5]

Other Christmas historians have made similar observations. Elizabeth H. Pleck notes of early settlers, "In colonial America Christmas was often celebrated as a drunken festival of carousing, begging, overeating, and masquerading,"[6] while Penne L. Restad writes, "'Frolicking,' the name many gave to this sort of boisterous Christmas and New Year's fun, could be found throughout the colonies."[7]

Even in colonial America, carnival fostered a more open expression of sexuality. "Life returned to normal when Christmas ended," notes Pleck, "except perhaps that a few unmarried girls had been made pregnant and many of the mischiefmakers had had too much to drink."[8] Nissenbaum notes that premarital pregnancies became more common near the middle of the 1700s in the

New England region, and "There was a 'bulge' in the number of births in the months of September and October—meaning that sexual activity peaked during the Christmas season."[9] It seems unsurprising that many Puritans objected to Christmas and New Year's festivals in England and America.

The initial Puritan objection to Christmas rested on theological ground: since the Bible never mentioned Jesus's birthday, there was no reason to celebrate it. Christmas was just another work day, the exception being when Christmas Day fell on the Sabbath, the primary holy day for the Puritans. Working on Christmas Day also provided a way to keep men and women out of mischief. Boston Minister Cotton Mather wrote in his journal in 1711, "I hear of a number of young people of both sexes, belonging, many of them, to my flock, who have had on the Christmas-night, this last week, a Frolic, a reveling feast, and Ball. . . . [T]he Feast of Christ's Nativity is spent in Reveling, Dicing, Carding, Masking, and in all Licentious Liberty . . . by Mad Mirth, by long Eating, by hard Drinking, by lewd Gaming, by rude Reveling."[10]

It is noted in both Nissenbaum's history and Leigh Eric Schmidt's *Consumer Rites* that middle-class Americans finally put an end to this more public, reveling version of Christmas during the early 1800s. Beginning in the 1820s, the middle class worked hard to create a family-oriented Christmas centered on children and gift exchange. The rudeness of carousing—door-to-door wassailing and street parties—offended the manners of the middle class and disrupted holiday shopping for merchants. Furthermore, the older calendar based on agriculture and the seasons disrupted the new industrial order. Lengthy festivals interrupted regular work patterns and, because of the excess of alcohol, continued to disrupt work after the festival had ended. "In the face of the economic and industrial rationalization that transformed early modern Europe and America," cultural historian Schmidt writes, "holidays looked decidedly backwards."[11]

It would be easy to gain the impression that Christmas misrule and carnival had no place within a family holiday that catered to middle-class Americans after the 1820s. To an extent, this was true; generally speaking, public or extroverted holiday celebrations based on excess were discouraged and repressed.

Still, excess was difficult to eradicate and balance because so many aspects of Christmas—even within a family-centered Christmas—were excessive in themselves. Christmas dinners, for instance, were a time for the family to overindulge in turkey, ham, and all the fixings, while alcohol—wine, eggnog, and distilled spirits—was seemingly more acceptable (or at least more readily available) during the Christmas season. With holiday kissing under the mistletoe, feasting on plum pudding, and toasting one another's good health, a fine line lay between seasonal celebrating and glut, between innocent seasonal indulgence and pleasure for pleasure's sake.

While these domestic aspects of excess may be explained as an acceptable and controlled (or conservative) version of carnival, carnival also survived in other forms. Middle-class Americans may have dominated the modern interpretation of Christmas, but it was apparently impossible to eliminate every form of carnival from the holiday. As Nissenbaum notes, "[O]dd residual pockets of resistance to a domestic Christmas remain even to this day, as vestiges of carnival behavior."[12]

One place that carnival survived was within music, maintaining its greatest strength in folk and underground cultures, though also entering popular culture in a watered-down form. Burke notes of European carnival that "Songs with double meanings were not only permitted at this time, but were virtually obligatory."[13] Nissenbaum has suggested that in more modern times the blues continued to offer a carnival version of an American Christmas. "African-American Christmas music is still largely associated with . . . carnival behavior—at least in *the blues*, that quintessential African-American genre."[14] Looking at the lyrics of a number of recorded blues songs that emphasized sensual pleasure, he notes, "In addition, all of these Christmas blues are in part *directed at* the conventional domestic Christmas ritual, a ritual they manage to transform into a kind of joyous sacrilege."[15]

Carnival Songs

The idea of carnival, however, was difficult to transfer into the mainstream American Christmas celebration without dilution. Within the winter holiday and the narrower confines of the American Christmas song, material focusing on nostalgia, children, and charity created a consensus within the mainstream during the 1940s and 1950s. Values centered on the family, home ownership, and material well-being had been woven into the textures of the American Christmas song. The lyrics and music of these songs likewise supported the equally important—though harder to pin down—ideals of democracy, freedom, and equality. Carnivalesque songs expressed little concern over these traditions and ideas and often seemed to deride them.

Nothing within the Christmas song category, however, prohibited romance or considered romance, in some fashion, to be a threat. Romance was perhaps the most common song type within popular music. Even within the Christmas tradition, the full lyric of "Jingle Bells"—written by James Pierpont in 1857—connected romance with a sleigh ride (though "Jingle Bells" was originally written for Thanksgiving). In the second verse, the singer takes Miss Fannie Bright for a sleigh ride, only to have the horse overturn the sleigh. In the last verse, the listener is invited to "Go it while you're young / Take the girls tonight / And sing a sleighing song." Romantic imagery, it seemed, could be spun out of the winter season just as easily as spring and summer.

Within the boundaries of romantic Christmas songs, elements of carnival (carnival-light) could be inserted, just as these elements were inserted into popular songs during the 1940s and 1950s. The question was how to balance these elements against the demands of the record label, the taste of the average listener, and the oversight of public censors. The idea, as Dennis R. Hall notes of *Playboy* magazine's holiday issues, was a "civilized sort of misrule."[16] There were also rare moments when a carnival-enhanced song slipped into the mainstream without anyone noticing, but these moments were short-lived. For mainstream America, carnival-light remained the order of the day through the mid-1950s, when all hell broke loose in the form of a rock-and-roll Christmas.

"Winter Wonderland" (1934)

Most carnivalesque songs that entered the mainstream between 1934 and 1950 were carnival-light, hinting at and suggesting sensuality but never spelling it out. In a song like "Winter Wonderland," romance is nigh as lovers explore an open landscape filled with snow, new birds, and sleigh bells. This innocent intermingling of winter and romance naturally culminates with the snowman dubbed Parson Brown, suggesting—along with the song's later

FIGURE 4.3. Carl Hassmann, "Puck Christmas, 1905," 1905. Photomechanical print: offset, color. Library of Congress.

allusion to promises made—that the lovers will marry in the near future. While the couple seems to be unaccompanied by chaperones, there is never the suggestion that their solitude is in any way improper.

In most recorded versions, the opening section of "Winter Wonderland" (an introductory verse as in "Santa Claus Is Comin' to Town" and "White Christmas") has been removed. Because the opening is very specific about the focus of the song—a romantic couple wandering in a snowy landscape at night—its loss helps obscure the central subject of the wandering couple.

Even without direct pointers from the opening verse, however, "Winter Wonderland" evokes romance through a frosty dreamland where people seem dazed by a mingling of seasonal beauty and personal feelings for one other. One thing that may be easy to forget—since the song offers such a lovely picture of the outdoor winter landscape—is that the song's vignettes occur at night. This dreamy quality is reflected in Johnny Mercer and the Pied Pipers' slow-moving arrangement of "Winter Wonderland" from 1947 (recalling the equally dreamy arrangement of "Let It Snow! Let it Snow! Let It Snow!" by Vaughn Monroe in 1945). Bells and light brass, followed by a smoothly orchestrated backdrop, lead the way for the Pied Pipers' absorbed reverie of the opening lines.

It might be easy to view Mercer and the Pied Pipers' version as nostalgic, since its pacing and relaxed delivery easily remind one of songs like "White Christmas," "I'll Be Home for Christmas," and "Have Yourself a Merry Little Christmas." This is perhaps even truer when it is listened to in the present, some sixty-five years after it was recorded. But the lovers are lost in a dream of the present, not the past, a dream neither wistful nor nostalgic. They have become part of the landscape they inhabit, a wonderland complete unto itself. Within the world of the song, even the sound of sleigh bells—reflected by the bells in the Mercer version—and glistening of the snow seem to be happening in slow motion. Within the spell of the moment, "Winter Wonderland" evokes the early stages of love where two people, caught up in the moment, create a world unto themselves.

Many of these elements lose force in more upbeat versions of "Winter Wonderland," as with Perry Como's bubbly recording of the song from 1946. While the lyrics are mostly the same, Como's version is more celebratory, placing more emphasis on

FIGURE 4.4. *Christmas in Connecticut,* 1945. Dennis Morgan and Barbara Stanwyck. By permission of Warner Bros./Photofest.

his buoyant vocal and the boisterous music than the lyrics. The radical difference in pacing between these versions essentially creates two interpretations, though arguably Mercer's take provides a more seamless fit between lyrics and music. Como's version revels in the winter landscape and the joy of the season, Mercer's in the feelings of the two lovers, lost in a magical landscape reflecting their emotions.

The overall romantic import of "Winter Wonderland" becomes much clearer when the opening verse is added (and neither Como's nor Mercer's versions include it). Here, an omniscient narrator sets the stage for the scene that will unfold, sketching the snow-covered landscape, a starlit night sky, and a couple enthralled with one another despite the chilly weather. Love, the narrator says, is not limited to a particular climate or season; as the young lovers walk and dream of the future, a winter setting is as good as any. As the more familiar opening of "Winter Wonderland" begins with talk of sleigh bells, this brief recitation has cued the listener on how to hear the song: it is about two people in love, exploring a wintry scene together.

We know very little else about the couple. They are alone at night without chaperones, and we assume—because the subject of marriage is spoken of later in the song—that they are unmarried. We may even assume that they are young, but the lyric is never specific. In the last verse of "Winter Wonderland," the couple—finished with their outdoor winter frolic—sits beside the fire, dreaming of the future. Part of this dream seems to refer to whatever exchanges of feelings the couple made, and while these are never spelled out in the song, it seems clear that they point back to Parson Brown: in the future, the couple plans to marry. While it is easy to read a sensuous undercurrent into the lyric (the couple is alone, they have decided to get married), "Winter Wonderland" remains mostly proper by the promise of marriage. If winter romance leads to marriage and family, the song works well within the overall philosophy of the mainstream Christmas song. Still, "Winter Wonderland" never mentions Christmas; its only concern is the romance of a couple during the winter season.

Romantic Christmas songs would have had one popular culture precedent before 1945: Christmas movies. In 1942, *Holiday Inn* helped establish the holiday movie as "White Christmas" had helped establish the popular holiday song. Most Christmas movies that appeared between 1942 and 1954, from *It's a Wonderful Life* (1946) to *Miracle on 34th Street* (1947) to *White Christmas* (1954), featured a romance regardless of the primary topic of the film.

In *Christmas in Connecticut* (1945), Elizabeth Lane (Barbara Stanwyck) is a magazine columnist who presents herself as a married mother who lives on a farm in Connecticut. While she espouses the spiritual pleasures of rural life in her column, in reality she is single and lives in a posh apartment in New York City. When the magazine's owner (unaware of her deceit) asks her to host a Connecticut Christmas for American soldier Jefferson Jones (Dennis Morgan), she temporarily moves into a friend's house, outfitting it with a husband and baby, to fulfill her role. Naturally within the romantic comedy genre, Lane and Jones fall for one another. But since he believes she is married, and since she must continue the deceit (the magazine owner has also joined them for the weekend), they are kept at a distance.

In an extended scene, Lane and Jones leave a Christmas party to walk outside, entering their own winter wonderland (they are followed, unbeknownst to either of them, by the magazine owner, who eventually falls into a snow bank). After Jones has pointed out that Lane's shoes are inadequate for walking in the snow, he talks her into sitting on a horse-drawn sleigh. "Where should we go?" he asks her. "Where do you generally go," she replies, "in your dreams?"[17] The horse, which is not tied, begins to pull the couple through a lovely night-time landscape of fields and lightly populated woods. Jones suggests turning back, but Lane insists that they continue. Sitting close together, looking into one another's eyes as they speak of the future they wish for but can never have, they are as lost in the magical night as the couple in "Winter Wonderland."

Perhaps it was the romantic nature of "Winter Wonderland" or perhaps the serious nature of the song's lyrics (marriage) that led music publisher Bregman, Vocco, and Conn, Inc., to print a new version of "Winter Wonderland" in 1947 (this was the earliest alteration of the 1934 lyric I was able to trace). On the 1947 sheet music, the cover proclaims, "This edition includes the original lyric and a new children's lyric."[18] While the first verse (minus the rarely performed opening section) of both the adults' and children's versions remain the same, the children's second verse finds the new bird no longer singing of love: the bird is merely singing. The snowman that appears in the bridge is transformed from a minister into a circus clown, and the promises made during the last verse are exchanged for frolicking like Eskimos. In the children's version of the song, there is no longer a context to understand the nonincluded opening section (the verse that spelled out the romantic nature of the song); "Winter Wonderland" has segued from a romantic winter interlude to a seasonal song about playing in the snow.

Over time, however, the distinction between the two versions became less clear, with singers like Johnny Mathis (in 1958) simply connecting both versions, providing the song with an extra verse and an extra chorus. Furthermore, Mathis adds the rarely used opening section in the middle of the song, assuring that the spirit of the original version of "Winter Wonderland" remained intact. Nothing, after all, prohibited lovers from making two snowmen, one a parson and the other a circus clown; and nothing prohibited the lovers from both frolicking like Eskimos and keeping promises of a future marriage. The children's version of "Winter Wonderland" had undercut the adult themes of romance, love, and marriage, crafting a lyric more suitable perhaps for grade-schoolers and more in line with governing Christmas themes. Romance, however, stubbornly persisted, claiming its corner in the holiday celebration.

"Let It Snow! Let it Snow! Let It Snow!" (1945)

First issued as a single by Vaughn Monroe and the Norton Sisters in 1945, "Let It Snow" picked up where "Winter Wonderland" left off. This early collaboration between Sammy Cahn and Jule Styne was much simpler and more straightforward than "Winter Wonderland," narrowing the surrounding distractions to focus on the song's couple: no opening section is needed to clarify the song's romantic subject matter. Monroe and the Norton Sisters' version of the song peaked at number one on the pop charts on December 22, 1945; the following year three other acts, Woody Herman, Connee Boswell and Russ Morgan, and Bob Crosby, charted with "Let It Snow."

The lyric of "Let It Snow" is divided into two simple counterparts: the inside and the outside, the warmth of the fire and the cold of the snowstorm. The first two lines set up this contrast ("frightful" weather, a "delightful" fire), while the first two lines of the second verse provide an echo: the storm shows no signs of letting up, so the couple might as well utilize the fire to make popcorn. While the weather may work as a convenient excuse (the couple seems in no hurry to part), it also helps to isolate them further from the world around them.

The lyric of "Let It Snow" also reinforces the romantic nature of the couple's meeting. They seem (like the couple in "Winter Wonderland") to be alone and under no obligation to be anywhere else. In the second stanza the lights have been turned down, and there is anticipation—when the couple goes home—of the warmth of holding each other tight (like the warmth of the fire) and a goodnight kiss (maybe also suggested in the word "goodbying"). If "Winter Wonderland" is a romance highlighted by the outdoors and seasonal scenery, then "Let It Snow" is a quieter drama highlighted by a dwelling's interior and a crackling fire.

The bridge to "Let It Snow" reassures the listener that the spell that the couple has fallen under for the evening will eventually be broken. At some point, the couple will kiss goodnight and go home. While the storm serves as a pretext, then, it is never so bad that the couple cannot go home. While the song's bridge seems to settle the matter of propriety—the couple, while perhaps caught up in the moment, will go home—"Let It Snow" never broaches the subject of marriage. Indeed, the song focuses on a couple sharing time together beside the fireplace on a stormy winter's night. During the third verse, love is mentioned, but the listener has no idea how serious the relationship might be. More than love, "Let It Snow" seems to be about the pleasure of the moment, a respite when two lovers find themselves alone and in each other's arms, ensconced in a cozy interior while the snow piles up outside.

FIGURE 4.5. *Kiss Me, Stupid*, 1964. Dean Martin and Kim Novak. By permission of Lopert Pictures/Photofest.

The song never answers whether the couple has purposely gone out into the storm or whether the snow has caught them by surprise. One of the two has brought popcorn, so the meeting does seem to have been planned. But where are they? Since the narrator speaks of going home in the song's bridge, the couple seems to have met somewhere else, but where that might be is left to the listener's imagination. "Let It Snow" is also unspecific about how the couple arrived and how they are going home. Since the narrator wishes for his love to hold him/her tight while going home, one might guess that they are either walking or perhaps riding in a horse-drawn sleigh.

Like "Winter Wonderland," "Let It Snow" never mentions Christmas, and while the song is filled with holiday imagery—snow, a fireplace, and popcorn—these items mostly serve as a backdrop. Also like "Winter Wonderland," "Let It Snow" is about a couple caught up in the moment, using the excuse of winter weather to steal away. While "Let It Snow" could be interpreted as a song about a young couple in a love affair that may eventually lead (as in "Winter Wonderland") to marriage, it could just as easily be interpreted as a song about romance by the fireplace. Unlike "Winter Wonderland," "Let It Snow" places emphasis on the closeness and sensuality of the couple. In "Winter Wonderland," the couple is lost in the depth of their feelings for one another; in "Let It Snow," the couple is lost in the physicality of the moment. While the couple in "Let It Snow" may feel the same about one another as the couple in "Winter Wonderland," "Let It Snow" is about passion and desire, not love.

Despite this emphasis on physical sensation and sensuality, "Let It Snow" seemed to fit well within the growing Christmas canon. Perhaps, as Albert J. Menendez and Shirley C. Menendez note in *Christmas Songs Made in America*, the song maintains an old-fashioned stance toward the romantic couple. "The lyrics have a certain pre-1960s innocence about them, referring to goodnight kisses, parting for the night, and popping corn. Delicacy and charm characterize the four brief stanzas."[19]

This interpretation, however, could be expanded by considering how the singer of "Let It Snow" might change the song's interpretation: might the song, performed by a singer known for his or her sex appeal, take on a less innocent meaning? In the version by Vaughn Monroe and the Norton Sisters from 1945, the song unfurls with lackadaisical allure. The lyric is underpinned by a smart vocal arrangement featuring exchanges between the male lead (Monroe) and the female chorus (the Norton Sisters). The use of both male and female voices, separately and entwined, also reinforces the harmony of the couple on this evening's escapade. Monroe's version provides a familiar musical backdrop, perhaps recalling or evoking the big band era of the previous ten years. In this fashion, Monroe and the Norton Sisters offer an enjoyable, though conservative, reading of "Let It Snow," adding nothing that would cause the listener to imagine anything more than a brief romantic interlude.

This conservative reading of "Let It Snow," however, is only one interpretation, and not necessarily how the song would have been read in 1945. Today, Vaughn Monroe's recording of "Let It Snow," with its orchestrated soundscape and easygoing pacing, may strike many listeners as old-fashioned and innocent (and again, even nostalgic). In his own time, however, Monroe was known by phrases like "the baritone with muscles;" he was a handsome singer with a masculine vocal style. In his own day, then, Monroe performed a romantic song that fitted his public image. While it may still be easy to interpret Monroe's version as innocent and old-fashioned, considering the song's relaxed cadence and the singer's vocal approach, the presence of star power had the potential to push the lyric in new directions.

Likewise, it may be easy to see how Dean Martin's version of "Let It Snow" from *A Winter Romance* in 1959 might have shifted the lyric's emphasis. Martin's personality/persona added an element that pushed the song beyond the lyric sheet. Described by one newspaper as "America's untamed version of Perry Como,"[20] Martin's reputation as a sex symbol, movie star, and member of the Rat Pack becomes intertwined with his recording of "Let It

Snow." Writing in the *Beaver Valley Times* in 1959 William Ewald notes, "Martin is very hot property right now and it's not difficult to see why. Like his buddy, Frank Sinatra, he oozes a kind of eccentric appeal: A loose-jointed masculinity coupled with a dollop of naughty small boy."[21]

Even the cover of *A Winter Romance* shows Martin holding one woman while flirting with another. With a ski lodge in the background, the winter scene is a place for a new kind of romance that seems nonchalant about commitment and marriage. It is a "winter romance," after all, and there is no reason for it to be any different (save the weather) from a summer romance. Martin incorporated a number of similar-themed songs on *A Winter Romance*, including "Baby, It's Cold Outside" and "It Won't Cool Off." Martin included no religious material, perhaps because "O Little Town of Bethlehem" would have seemed as out of place on *A Winter Romance* as "Baby, It's Cold Outside" would have seemed on a Bing Crosby album. While the lyrical content of both Monroe's and Martin's versions of "Let It Snow" remained the same, Martin's public persona as a gambler, rambler, and leading lady's man potentially added a risqué quality that assured a less innocent rendering of the song.

"Baby, It's Cold Outside" (1949)

If "Let It Snow" picks up where "Winter Wonderland" left off, "Baby, It's Cold Outside" seems to restart with another, more modern couple. A great deal of the pre-1960s innocence that Albert and Shirley Menendez speak of in "Let It Snow" has also dissipated. Here, while a singer like Dean Martin may push the suggestive language of "Baby, It's Cold Outside" further than a singer

FIGURE 4.6. *Neptune's Daughter*, 1949. Esther Williams and Ricardo Montalbán. By permission of MGM/Photofest.

like Vaughn Monroe, the suggestion hangs in the air either way. If there is little doubt that the couple will return home separately for the night in "Let It Snow," this is never clear in "Baby, It's Cold Outside." Like the couple in "Let It Snow," the couple in "Baby, It's Cold Outside" is alone, caught between warm interiors and winter storms, caught between staying longer (and going further) or going home (and reducing public suspicion of hanky-panky). Unlike "Let It Snow" where the couple seems to be of one mind, however, seduction seems to be the objective in "Baby, It's Cold Outside."

Like "Winter Wonderland" and "Let It Snow," nothing about "Baby, It's Cold Outside" relates specifically to Christmas. In fact, the song was originally used in *Neptune's Daughter* (1949), an Esther Williams romantic comedy released during the summer. The song appears twice in the movie, first sung by Williams and Ricardo Montalbán and then back-to-back by Red Skelton and Betty Garrett; the lack of any bad weather is part of the song's humor within the film. Five versions of "Baby, It's Cold Outside" charted between May and July in 1949, an unusual time for a song associated with winter and Christmas to become a hit.

"Baby, It's Cold Outside" diverges from most other Christmas songs of the era in several ways. Many Christmas songs written between 1932 and 1963 were quite short, leading singers to repeat verses and choruses; in some versions of "White Christmas" and "Let It Snow," the lyric is finished halfway through the song and repeated after an instrumental break. "Baby, It's Cold Outside" has more words than "Winter Wonderland" and "Let It Snow" combined. Because the lyrics form a dialog, "Baby, It's Cold Outside" usually (though not always) demands a duet; of the five versions that charted in 1949, four were duets and one, a country music parody, was sung by Homer and Jethro with June Carter. With the barrage of lyrical dialog and two distinct lyric sections calling for a duet, "Baby, It's Cold Outside" resembles a scene from a romantic comedy (like *Neptune's Daughter*) filled with snappy verbal wit.

"Baby, It's Cold Outside" was also a rare comic holiday song tailored for an adult audience. As the Christmas song developed during the 1940s and 1950s, the novelty song—"All I Want for Christmas (Is My Two Front Teeth)" (1948), "I Saw Mommy

Kissing Santa Claus" (1953), and "Nuttin' for Christmas" (1955)—was primarily aimed toward children. "Baby, It's Cold Outside," however, injected sophisticated dialog between a romantically involved man (or a man *trying* to become romantically involved) and woman, a far cry from "The Chipmunk Song" (1958).

What seems like mild suggestiveness in Martin's version of "Let It Snow" becomes the underlying drive of "Baby, It's Cold Outside." Here, the lyric clearly centers on seduction, with the man (or whoever is singing what lyricist Frank Loesser termed the "wolf" part) attempting to convince the woman (the "mouse") to stay with him longer. With each of her objections he reminds her that it is cold outside. While the wolf is clearly the seducer in "Baby, It's Cold Outside," he is playing an agreed upon role. As in a romantic comedy, the couple enacts a battle between the sexes, with traditional male and female parts. The male pursues, attempting to seduce the female, while the female resists, or at least gives the impression of resisting. The battle between the sexes, then, is a game between the mouse and the wolf.

While the couples in "Winter Wonderland" and "Let It Snow" show little concern about what others may think, the woman in "Baby, It's Cold Outside" does at least express surface concern with propriety. She tells the man that her mother will worry, her father will pace the floor, her sister will be suspicious, and her brother will be waiting; likewise, the neighbors might wonder what they are doing, and the next day, there is bound to be loose talk. While it remains unclear how much weight she attaches to what people will think, she places her emphasis on decorum, not virtue. In other words, if she is worried about her own virtue, she never says so. It seems more likely that her objections are part of the mouse-wolf game the couple is playing. In this fashion, "Baby,

It's Cold Outside" suggests that fooling around and sex are less moral questions, even from the mouse's point of view, than ones of appearance.

As comic material, "Baby, It's Cold Outside" may have seemed an unpromising song to parody, but one was recorded by country comedy team Homer and Jethro with June Carter in 1949. The song is purposely over the top, filled with country humor. Instead of staying for half a drink more, for instance, the woman remains for half a jug more; instead of imagining her father pacing the floor, she imagines him picking up his shotgun. While this version of "Baby, It's Cold Outside" may have been funny to many listeners, it also offered an antidote to the suggestiveness of the original version. The song's content, undermined by country comedy, has been rendered safe for more conservative rural America. No one seemed to consider, however, that the idea of two men attempting to corner one woman was rather unusual in its own right.

It is easy to wonder in retrospect why "Baby, It's Cold Outside" was able to get past the public censors in 1949 and throughout the 1950s. One can speculate that the song was comic, which helped lighten the overall import. Because it evoked a romantic scene in a romantic comedy and enacted a typical battle between the sexes, the theme would have been familiar. Within *Neptune's Daughter*, the version of "Baby, It's Cold Outside" by Red Skelton (Jack Spratt) and Betty Garret (Betty Barrett) is purposefully humorous, reversing the man's and woman's roles. In the movie, it is this rendition that ends more suggestively with Garret turning out the light at the end of the song. Even the more serious version of "Baby, It's Cold Outside" by Ricardo Montalbán (José O'Rourke) and Esther Williams (Eve Barrett) is lightly comic, undercutting any gravity that viewers may have associated with the subject of seduction. With no snow or bad weather, a reversal of wolf-mouse roles in one version, and broad comic appeal, perhaps "Baby, It's Cold Outside" seemed nonthreatening to a general audience.

Outside the context of *Neptune's Daughter*, however, the very nature of "Baby, It's Cold Outside" may have dampened the song's reception for some listeners. One listener's rejoinder to "Baby, It's Cold Outside" was reprinted in *Life*. Responding to a story about the song's author, Frank Loesser, Thomas B. Congdon Jr. of New Haven, Connecticut, wrote "The Fine Art of the Hit Tune": "When Author Havemann points with pride / To trash like *Baby, It's Cold Outside* / And shudders at the open vice / Of *I Love You* set to *Three Blind Mice*, / I fear I'd say, were I assessor, / The greater evil is the Loesser."[22] A non-American critic of "Baby, It's Cold Outside" was visiting from Iraq in 1951. Attending a church dance, future Egyptian author Sayyid Qutb was surprised when the minister chose "Baby, It's Cold Outside" for a couples' dance:

> And the Father chose. He chose a famous American song called, "But Baby, It's Cold Outside," which is composed of a dialogue between a boy and a girl returning from their evening date. The boy took the girl to his home and kept her from leaving. She entreated him to let her return home, for it was getting late, and her mother was waiting but every time she would make an excuse, he would reply to her with this line: but baby, it's cold outside!
>
> And the minister waited until he saw people stepping to the rhythm of this moving song, and he seemed satisfied and contented. He left the dance floor for his home, leaving the men and the women to enjoy this night in all its pleasure and innocence![23]

Whatever concerned the public and the censors over the content of "Baby, It's Cold Outside," the suggestive content of lyrics and the delivery of those lyrics would be pushed much further during the mid-1950s.

The Lord of Misrule

After World War II, carnival temporarily erupted in the form of the Christmas office party. As in older celebrations of the season, the office party turned the normal order upside down; everyone, for the duration of the party—boss, secretaries, managers, and clerks—were on the same social level. "The occasion is that great leveler, the office Christmas party, an antidote to the social formality which ranks between a few discreet cocktails and a free-for-all fight," wrote *Life* magazine in 1948. The celebration was fueled by alcohol, revelry, and—rumors often reported—licentiousness. "By the 1950s and early 1960s," notes Susan Waggoner, "so many office parties had become such bacchanalian affairs that magazines addressed them as a serious social threat."[24] *Playboy* included cartoons referencing office parties, one of which even featured a group of elves reveling at their North Pole workshop. While Santa seems perplexed at the out-of-control party (dancing and drinking), one elf explains to Santa, "And what's wrong with us little elves having a Christmas party?!"[25]

If the office party seemed like a crack in the façade of the postwar social order and decorum, rock and roll would seem like an earthquake. While pre-1963 rock and roll may seem the essence of innocence in retrospect, with its focus on sock hops, drive-ins, jukeboxes, hamburger joints, and '57 Chevys (captured in the opening verses of Don McLean's "American Pie" and throughout

George Lucas's *American Graffiti*), many Eisenhower-era adults viewed rock and roll as a threat to all things American.

In the April 18, 1955, issue of *Life*, the magazine considered the generational conflict that had formed around the music. "The nation's teen-agers," *Life* wrote, "are dancing their way into an enlarging controversy over rock 'n roll."[26] *Life's* response to rock and roll came so early in the music's development that they paused to offer a basic definition of the new music: "Rock 'n Roll is both music and dance. The music has a rhythm often heavily accented on the second and fourth beat."[27] The title of one *Life* article, "A Question of Questionable Lyrics," pointed toward part of the underlying problem from middle America's point of view. "[P]arents and police were startled by other rock 'n roll records' words, which were frequently suggestive and occasionally lewd."[28] These questionable lyrics, the raucous music, and the dancing, *Life* noted, left parents wondering exactly what their kids were up to at rock and roll parties. Rock and roll parties were like office parties, then, except for one significant difference: they seemed to involve an entire generation of teenagers. In both situations, though, there always seemed to be a danger—as with carnival—of losing control.

Many believed that rock and roll, in the form of Elvis Presley, also threatened to deconstruct or simply destroy the Christmas song as it had formed between 1942 and the mid-1950s. As material for the holiday gristmill expanded between the early 1940s and mid-1950s, the Christmas song had become a yearly staple of radio playlists and industry charts. All of these songs, evoking nostalgia, anticipation, selfless giving, and romance, reflected mainstream American values in relation to Christmas. While the romantic holiday song may have hinted at carnival, there had been clear limits. Because of these limits, "Winter Wonderland" and "Let It Snow" were easy to enfold within popular music without endangering mainstream holiday values. By following a loose template measured against middle-class social values, the American Christmas song had become an accepted, predictable, profitable, and conservative category of popular music.

This changed abruptly in 1957 with the release of *Elvis' Christmas Album*. As the prime mover and shaker of rock and roll, Elvis Presley's holiday songs seemed to hold the promise of undermining the fundamental values of an American Christmas (just as his other music seemed to hold the promise of undermining *all* American values). With his swagger, swaying hips, and youthfulness, Presley's rock and roll Christmas turned Bing Crosby, Perry Como, and Nat King Cole inside-out.

The original issue of *Elvis' Christmas Album* delivered an odd mixture of secular material, traditional carols, and spirituals, a hodgepodge barely held together under the umbrella of Christmas. On side one, Presley focused on secular material, including "Santa Claus Is Back in Town," "White Christmas," "Here Comes Santa Claus," "I'll Be Home for Christmas," "Blue Christmas," and "Santa Bring My Baby Back (To Me)"; on side two, he concentrated on carols, including "O Little Town of Bethlehem" and "Silent Night," and four spirituals, "Peace in the Valley," "I Believe," "Take My Hand, Precious Lord," and "It Is No Secret (What God Can Do)" (the spirituals were taken from an EP released earlier in 1957, *Peace in the Valley*, and perhaps worked as filler). In retrospect, the tracking itself is bizarre. Within the span of one album, Presley attempted to stitch together sexualized blues ("Santa Claus Is Back in Town"), sacred secular songs ("White Christmas"), solemn carols ("Silent Night"), and traditional spirituals ("Peace in the Valley").

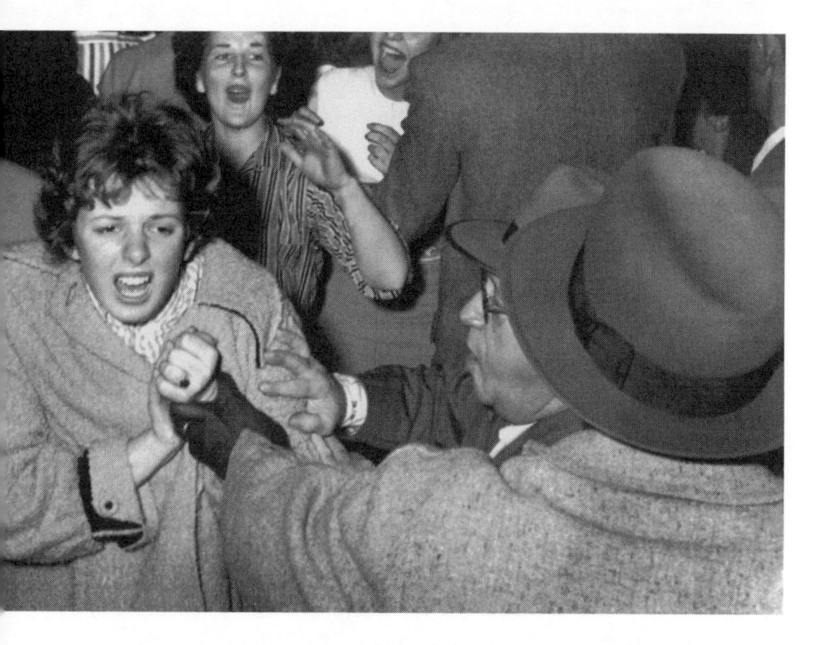

FIGURE 4.7. "Elvis Presley Fans," 1950s. By permission of Photofest.

For Presley fans, neither the tracking nor the Christmas theme was of great importance: it was an Elvis album and that was enough. For many nonfans, however, the combination was too much. In a *Billboard* article about the album, one disc jockey told the magazine, "No, I won't play it. That's like having Tempest Storm (stripper) give gifts to my kids."[29]

Within the swirling rejection of *Elvis' Christmas Album* was Irving Berlin's personal vendetta, aimed squarely at Presley's version of "White Christmas." If the popular holiday song of the last fifteen years had provided an essential soundtrack to an American Christmas, then Berlin's "White Christmas" was the most sacred of artifacts. It served as a broad testament to American ideals, an article of faith while claiming no specific religious heritage. By recording "White Christmas," Presley and RCA had struck at the heart of all things considered sacred within an American Christmas during the 1940s and 1950s, threatening to knock it down or rip it up with the debauchery of carnival. The physical body—sensual, in motion, and in the moment—would undermine the higher aspirations of the spirit.

Berlin mounted a campaign against Presley's "White Christmas," instructing staff to contact radio stations and ask them not to play the song. Whether a coincidence or as a result of Berlin's campaign, station manager Mel Bailey of KEX in Portland, Oregon, fired disk jockey Al Priddy for playing "White Christmas," noting the "treatment of the song was in extremely poor taste."[30] In the *Tri City Herald,* Bailey sharpened his critique: "Presley gives it ["White Christmas"] a rhythm and blues interpretation. It doesn't seem to me to be in keeping with the intent of the song."[31] Berlin's personal issue spoke to a broader social one, a raw nerve that *Elvis' Christmas Album* exposed and then, from a mainstream American viewpoint, rudely poked. By thumbing his nose at pop music history and transforming holiday favorites into rock and roll discord, Presley unleashed a heavy dose of carnival into an American Christmas. In essence, Presley—whether he intended to or not—became the Lord of Misrule, bringing the same sexual abandon to Christmas that he had brought to popular music.

The hysteria of young girls emphasized both Presley's appeal and the broader social threat. In one story in the *St. Joseph's News-Press* from early 1957, the paper reported that "Thirteen girls, many wailing 'We want Elvis!' were carried to the first aid station during the rock 'n' roll singer's one-night Chicago program."[32] This was disturbing on any day, and perhaps more so when planted against the imagery of home and family during Christmas. When a young Santa Claus asked two fourteen-year-old girls what they wanted for Christmas in 1956, they replied, "Elvis Presley. Not a doll or a picture of him, but Elvis Presley, period."[33] The Reverend Carl E. Elgena cut to the chase, telling his congregation, "The belief in unholy pleasure has sent the morals of our nation down to rock bottom and the crowning addition to this day's corruption is Elvis Presleyism."[34]

After Presley was drafted at the beginning of 1958, the major record companies worked hard to convince the public that the carnival vision of Christmas (and rock and roll in general) had been no more than a bad dream. It was ironic that Dean Martin's *A Winter Romance* might appear fairly conservative in 1959, and that his version of "Baby, It's Cold Outside" may have actually worked as an antidote to Presley's sexually charged "Santa Claus Is Back in Town." Both Martin with *A Winter Romance* and Johnny Mathis with *Merry Christmas* (1958) served as acceptable versions of the 1950s sex symbol who performed Christmas music. Carnival, however, had a habit of reemerging. In 1964, seven years after the issue of *Elvis' Christmas Album*, RCA released "Blue Christmas" as a single for the first time. Presley's "Blue Christmas" climbed to number one on the recently established *Billboard* Christmas chart and continued to place consecutively through 1970.

FIGURE 5.1. "Remember the Poor: A Salvation Army Christmas Box," ca. 1903. Negative: glass, 8 × 10. Detroit Publishing Company; Library of Congress.

5

The Blues and Hard Times: An American Carol

Although this [the holidays] is a time when people are supposed to be happy, and many are, there are some for whom the expected happiness does not arrive. Lonely people, people without family or friends, feel lonelier than ever when they see celebrations going on all around them.

Norman E. Rosenthal, *Winter Blues*

Daddy'd get drunk ever' Christmas. . . . When he got home, Mommy got on him. . . . They'd have a cuss fight just as sure as he'd get drunk. They wasn't a Christmas that passed hardly that he didn't get drunk but through the other times he hardly ever did.

D. B. Dayton, *Foxfire 9*

I just don't understand Christmas, I guess. I might be getting presents and sending Christmas cards and decorating trees and all that, but I'm still not happy. I always end up feeling depressed.

Charlie Brown, *A Charlie Brown Christmas*

In 1973 John Prine included a lone Christmas song on his album *Sweet Revenge*. The title itself, "Christmas in Prison," may have led the listener unfamiliar with the singer to imagine a country music parody like Commander Cody's "Daddy's Drinking Up Our Christmas" (1972) or perhaps like the Youngsters' humorous and cautionary tale, "Christmas in Jail" (1956). But Prine had something more serious in mind: a desolate lyric from the point of view of a prisoner during the holiday season.

In addition to the social isolation of prison, the convict in "Christmas in Prison" speaks of his painful separation from someone he loves. The typical trappings of Christmas, special food, music, and snow, only increase the prisoner's homesickness. Unlike the narrators of "White Christmas" or "I'll Be Home for Christmas," the prisoner has no possibility of returning home for Christmas. His wait is described as "eternity," and even were he to be released, it would be impossible to guess what kind of homecoming awaited him. With a stripped folk arrangement accompanying Prine's sandpaper vocal, "Christmas in Prison" is as bleak as midwinter, a holiday lyric leaving little hope of redemption.

Songs focusing on the holiday blues and hard times expanded the Christmas conscience. Working against the backdrop of Charles Dickens's *A Christmas Carol* (1843), these songs touched on issues of social isolation and class. While it might have been agreeable to preserve the façade that Christmas was a happy time for all Americans, there seemed to be a need to recognize less hopeful holiday experiences. Some folks were lonely, separated from lovers, families, and friends, while others suffered from poverty, leaving them hungry, without proper shelter, and with no resources to celebrate a traditional American Christmas. Often, these two themes intermingled.

Christmas arrived once a year for both happy and dysfunctional families, for those who loved the holidays and those who wished for them to hurry by. The spirit of celebration and goodwill shared by many Americans only served to highlight how far others had fallen. Writing about the holiday blues in the *New Yorker Magazine* in December of 1967, Edwin Diamond noted, "Most Americans do indeed enjoy a merry Christmas. . . . But for a significant—and apparently increasing—number of people, Christmas is the worst of times. For them, this is the season of mishaps, depression and anxiety."[1]

If songs focusing on Christmas past were bathed in the warm glow of yesteryear, songs focusing on loneliness, hard times, and the holiday blues teetered on the brink of melancholy and dejection. Whereas nostalgia seemed to be a temporary state of mind that someone could fall in and out of, melancholy and dejection lingered; whereas nostalgia seemed to be a self-indulgent luxury, melancholy and dejection were dead ends. While there may have been room for hope—that your true love will hear your plea and return for Christmas, that you will find a new job and be able to provide Christmas gifts for your family, or that an unforeseen event will cause the vague feeling of dissatisfaction to dissipate—there was little room for cheerfulness until the loved one appeared, the job materialized, or the miracle arrived.

In its broadest sense, the holiday blues reflected a complaint that often remained undefined and open-ended. Partly self-absorbed, partly emanating from holiday overload, the holiday blues almost seemed un-American in the midst of the most joyful of holidays. Indeed, guilt over feeling the wrong way during the happiest time of year only intensified the holiday blues. Writing about changes in Christmas culture during the 1960s, Elizabeth Pleck notes:

> Psychiatrists—the "experts" of the postwar world—reported that the Christmastime emotions their patients experienced were melancholy, depression, and loneliness. . . . To some extent, the psychological problem of overexpectation followed by disappointment had been a theme in writing about Christmas since the nineteenth century, but the naming of the phenomenon, the "Christmas syndrome" or the "Dickens' syndrome," was new.[2]

In a narrower sense, however, the holiday blues could often be isolated and defined. While many complained of feeling "blah" or out of sorts, others experienced quantifiable life events such as job loss and romantic disappointment. In *The World Encyclopedia of Christmas*, Gerry Bowler offers a list of common complaints:

- loss of a loved one
- resentment of the commercialism of the season
- a sense of not belonging, stemming from membership in a religion that does not celebrate Christmas
- anger over not being able to afford gifts for one's family
- anger at seasonally induced weight gain or increase in indebtedness
- homelessness, friendlessness, or alienation from family or ethic group
- guilt at not being as happy as the ideal family depicted on television
- spouse saturation syndrome (too much of one's mate underfoot)
- separation at holiday-times from one's lover who is married to someone else[3]

The holiday blues, then, incorporated everything from the bad day to existential angst, from loneliness and sorrow to economic hardship. Later, some psychologists and psychiatrists attempted to simplify this plethora of complaints into seasonal affective disorder (SAD), a syndrome partly caused by low levels of light during the winter months. For many Americans, though, it was hard to shake a recurrent coincidence: call them what you will, these blues seemed to come and go with the Christmas season.

The blues and hard times may have been perennial themes in American culture, but they appeared to resonate more deeply during the Christmas holiday. During Christmas, the down-and-out, the jobless, and the downhearted were cut off from the communal holiday experience, whether that meant an inability to join in the good cheer or to participate in the bounty of the American Dream. If it seemed a patriotic obligation to partake in the emotional and material abundance of an American Christmas, nonparticipants became isolated outcasts, hoping for little more than sympathy and a handout.

These complaints seeped into the Christmas song after World War II. With a change of scenery, the ever popular breakup song was easily transformed into a Christmas breakup song (Charles Brown's "Please Come Home for Christmas"); likewise, it was easy to combine a romance gone bad with the holiday blahs (Joni Mitchell's "River"). In country songs about hard times, a change of seasonal scenery produced unemployed men who struggled through the winter months (Merle Haggard's "If We Make It Through December") and poor boys waiting for Santa Claus (Eddy Arnold's "Will Santy Come to Shanty Town"). Other popular performers, Simon and Garfunkel with "A Hazy Shade of Winter," Dan Fogelberg with "Same Old Lang Syne," and Dolly

Parton with "Hard Candy Christmas," offered various combinations of the holiday blues. The popular Christmas song may have been able to ignore the bleakness of a John Prine Christmas, but it would nonetheless recognize that for many people, the holidays were far from happy.

The Two Sides of *A Christmas Carol*

With its images of and attitudes toward the holiday blues and hard times, Charles Dickens's *A Christmas Carol* became one of the most lasting influences on the modern American Christmas. Yes, all may come out well in the end in Dickens's tale, just as it does in Hollywood, but Scrooge has to endure a great deal of emotional pain and experience a conversion before a happy ending can be produced. Within the book, both the holiday blues and hard times are reflected in and through the portrait of Scrooge, revealing him as an unkind miser *and* a lost and lonely soul; as a man who has turned business profit into a personal religion *and* as a man who is emotionally bankrupt. Scrooge is an unhappy, selfish bachelor, and as unhappy as he seems, he appears determined to remain that way.

The reader of *A Christmas Carol* knows Scrooge as a tight-fisted miser who repeats "Bah!" and "Humbug!" Partly because the "scrooge" character has become a staple of popular Christmas culture, we know—after meeting this character only briefly—how he will respond to the world around him. He is a man who coldly refuses to give to charity ("Are there no prisons?")[4]; he is unkind to both his employee, Bob Cratchit ("But I suppose you must have the whole day [for Christmas]. Be here all the earlier next morning!"),[5] and his nephew ("what reason have you to be

FIGURE 5.2. *Scrooge*, 1951. George Cole and Rona Anderson. By permission of United Artists/Photofest.

merry? You're poor enough").[6] He guards against even the smallest indulgences, preferring to live and work in chilly rooms instead of spending money for coal. In his words and habits, Scrooge is a walking, talking caricature of a miser and, as such, mostly unsympathetic. He is greedy and uncaring for humanity, bad qualities on any day but worse during the Christmas season.

One clear lesson that Scrooge learns after a series of ghostly visitations is one that his deceased partner, Jacob Marley, never learned: "'Business!' cried the [Marley's] Ghost, wringing its hands again, 'Mankind was my business. The common welfare was my business; charity, mercy, forbearance, and benevolence, were, all, my business. The dealings of my trade were but a *drop* of water in the comprehensive ocean of my business!'"[7] After his conversion, Scrooge amends his former neglect of mankind. He buys an oversized turkey and sends it to the Cratchit family ("It's twice the size of tiny Tim"),[8] presumably offers a large sum to a charitable organization ("'Lord bless me!' cried the gentleman, as if his breath were gone. 'My dear Mr. Scrooge, are you serious?'"),[9] and raises Bob Cratchit's salary ("I'll raise your salary, and endeavor to assist your struggling family").[10] Of his generous donation to charity Scrooge explains, "A great many back-payments are included in it, I assure you."[11] Scrooge learns a lesson that has become conventional Christmas wisdom: during the holidays, we should always remember those who have less. As historian Leigh Eric Schmidt notes, "To remember the poor was an obligation of the season."[12]

In the movement from penny pincher to generous patron of his employee and the poor, Scrooge's conversion reads like a straightforward morality play. Dickens improves his sketch of Scrooge considerably (and likewise deepens the resonance of *A Christmas Carol*) by also showing his isolated existence. Scrooge seems unaware of his loneliness at the beginning of *A Christmas Carol*; this is simply how he lives. We learn early in the book that even on Christmas Eve, Scrooge "took his melancholy dinner in his usual melancholy tavern."[13] He even lives as the sole occupant in a building "let out as offices."[14] His secluded existence stands in contrast to that of his nephew, who has a wife ("Why did you get married?" Scrooge asks his nephew. "Because I fell in love"),[15] and to that of Bob Cratchit, who has a large, vibrant family ("Then all the Cratchit family drew round the hearth, in what Bob Cratchit called a circle. . . . Bob proposed: 'A Merry Christmas to us all, my dears. God bless us!' Which all the family re-echoed").[16] While these descriptions of Scrooge's loneliness and isolation are important, they only lightly touch upon a more pressing issue: Scrooge, the lone miser, has neither wife nor children nor friends of his own. These details prepare the reader for a deeper rendering of a solitary man.

This lack of domestic warmth is highlighted when the Ghost of Christmas Past visits Scrooge, unveiling the saddest moments of his life (and perhaps the saddest moments in *A Christmas Carol*). Two successive passages revolve around a young Scrooge, at first as a boy at school and later as a young man making his way in the world. As Scrooge and the Ghost approach a school house in the first passage, the Ghost of Christmas Past offers: "'The school is not quite deserted,' said the Ghost. 'A solitary child, neglected by friends, is left still.' Scrooge said he knew it. And he sobbed."[17] The Ghost and Scrooge continue to a "mansion of dull red brick," where Scrooge is discovered, once again, alone. "It opened before them [a door], and disclosed a long, bare, melancholy room, made barer still by lines of plain deal forms and desks. At one of these a lonely boy was reading near a feeble fire; and Scrooge sat down upon a form, and wept to see his poor forgotten self as he had used to be."[18] Soon, another child enters the scene, Scrooge's sister coming to bring him home for Christmas. It is easy to gain the impression that young Scrooge has been sent away and that his father is unkind, though Dickens remains unspecific. While it may be easy for the reader to cheer for young Scrooge's homecoming, the words of his sister Fanny remain hanging in the air: "Father is so much kinder than he used to be, that home's like Heaven!"[19]

In *The Annotated Christmas Carol,* Michael Patrick Hearn draws correlations between these scenes and Dickens's own biography. For the passage noting "a lonely boy was reading," Hearn asserts, "This child was the boy Charles Dickens."[20] Noting the meeting between the young Scrooge and his sister, Hearn writes: "Although traditionally in English homes boys had far more advantages than girls did, Scrooge's father treated his sister far better than him; Dickens thought the same of his own family. He always resented that his parents sent Fanny Dickens to the Royal Academy of Music, while he had to drudge in Warren's Blacking warehouse."[21] Dickens uses these memories to enrich a portrait of social isolation, causing pity for Scrooge but also helping to explain his character.

Perhaps the saddest scene from the past in *A Christmas Carol,* and the portion of Scrooge's life that cannot be rectified, is the replay of his parting as a young man from his fiancée, Belle. Belle is described as "a fair young girl" wearing a "mourning-dress," with "tears, which sparkled in the light that shone out of the Ghost of Christmas Past."[22] While the mourning dress is never explained, it is possible that Belle, who does not have a dowry, has recently lost a parent. As a young man, Scrooge's fear of poverty and his pursuit of wealth seem to add an even greater sting to the distance that has grown between the two lovers: because of her lack of a dowry, Belle believes that Ebenezer, given a choice, would not choose her a second time. She tells him, "Another idol has displaced me [gold]; and if it can cheer and comfort you in time to come, as I would have tried to do, I have no just cause to grieve."[23] After Scrooge is unable to respond to these charges in any meaningful way, Belle releases him from the commitment of their relationship (since Scrooge's nephew marries for love, he seems to offer a portrait of Scrooge had he taken another path). She ends by offering what will become prophetic words: "You may—the memory of what is past half makes me hope you will—have pain in this. A very, very brief time, and you will dismiss the recollection of it, gladly, as an unprofitable dream, from which it happened well that you awoke. May you be happy in the life you have chosen!"[24] Now, from the distance of years, the memory of this scene is awakened once again, and Scrooge better understands his shortsightedness and what has been lost. Scrooge can make a choice to change his life (in the present), giving to the poor and considering his employee's needs, but he will have to live with the memories of the past. Both his father's mistreatment and his loneliness as a boy and his estrangement from and eventual loss of Belle are parts of his past that cannot be erased; both his mistreatment at the hands of others and his mistreatment of others remain stenciled in his consciousness.

Following in Dickens's shadow, American short-story writers, movie directors, and song writers would borrow, alter, and expand upon images and themes drawn from *A Christmas Carol*. While the basic imprint may have remained, these artists attempted to inscribe an American identity onto Scrooge's seasonal blues and English hard times.

One of the more illustrative and, over time, popular results was director Frank Capra's *It's a Wonderful Life* from 1946. In this reimagining of *A Christmas Carol*, the streets of London were traded for the small town of Bedford Falls, and the bustling urban masses were exchanged for a colorful mixture of immigrants, entrepreneurs, and Midwesterners; the swirling fog of an anonymous industrial city opened into the clean air of a factoryless hamlet populated with friendly neighbors; Dickens's portraits of the financial miser, good-natured nephew, and kind-hearted clerk made way for a host of characters borrowed from a Norman Rockwell *Saturday Evening Post* illustration. *It's a Wonderful Life* may tell the story of the dark night of one man's soul, but it does so against an

Americana backdrop quite at odds with the gloomy settings used for *A Christmas Carol.*

The most noticeable alteration in *It's a Wonderful Life,* and the one that helps conceal the source of its material, is the choice of protagonists: Jimmy Stewart's George Bailey has nothing in common with Scrooge. While Bailey may express bitterness at being isolated in Bedford Falls, he is an admirable character that everybody knows and everybody likes. He has sacrificed his dreams to help other people reach theirs and it seems that nearly everyone in Bedford Falls owes Bailey gratitude. Even while his original dreams of travel and working as an architect have been left unfulfilled, he has married the girl he loves, has started a family with her, and is president of the Building and Loan. The protagonist of *It's a Wonderful Life,* then, more closely resembles an Americanized Bob Cratchit, replacing his English counterpart's humility and subservience with an extroverted eagerness, an energetic "can do" spirit, and Protestant work ethic.

Since George Bailey is basically a good person, he has no need for three spirits to convince him to live a better life; he already believes that helping others, serving as a member of the community, and making personal sacrifices are virtuous. All he needs is one nondenominational angel to convince him that his life, even while many of his dreams remain unfulfilled, has really been wonderful.

Even while set within the comfort of small town America, *It's a Wonderful Life* provides a series of images haunted by the holiday blues. In an early scene in the movie, before Bailey is visited by the angel Clarence (Henry Travers), he exhibits his bottled-up frustration over the responsibilities that have chained him to Bedford Falls. In a scene with love interest Mary Hatch (Donna Reed), Bailey expresses an odd emotion for someone who is in

FIGURE 5.3. *It's a Wonderful Life,* 1946. Donna Reed and James Stewart. By permission of RKO/Photofest.

love: despair. He seems to understand that if he marries Hatch, who has just returned from college, he will never have a chance to leave Bedford Falls. As they huddle together around the phone to listen to friend Sam Wainwright (Frank Albertson) speak of the financial future of plastics, Bailey eventually breaks down, the phone is dropped, and he shouts at Hatch. The script describes his tone as speaking "fiercely." "Now you listen to me! I don't want any plastics! I don't want any ground floors, and I don't want to get married—ever—to anyone! You understand that? I want to do what *I* want to do. And you're . . . and you're . . ."[25]

George loves Mary, but his desperation is real. He will suppress his desire to see the world and he will make a compromise, but part of him remains very unhappy about it.

This scene deepens the ongoing split between Bailey's desire and his everyday reality, leaving an imprint that pushes beyond the seeming exterior of a young boy's daydreams: Bailey really wishes to lead a different life, but everything seems to conspire against him. The scene with Mary establishes the emotional desperation that simmers below the surface in Bailey, threatening to reemerge during a time of crisis.

This is exactly what happens at the climax of *It's a Wonderful Life*. Following an error at the Building and Loan that promises to bring shame and ruin on Bailey, he decides that he is worth more dead than alive. In a series of scenes—shouting at his uncle, begging for a bank loan, yelling at his children, breaking into tears, drinking in a barroom, wrecking his car, and standing on the bridge looking down into the river—Bailey displays an extreme case of the holiday blues. In the midst of these scenes, it is villain Henry S. Potter who seems to get in the last word, describing Bailey in a way he might (in his desperation) describe himself:

> Look at you. You used to be so cocky! You were going to go out and conquer the world! You once called me a warped, frustrated old man. What are you but a warped, frustrated young man? A miserable little clerk crawling in here on your hands and knees and begging for help. No securities—no stocks—no bonds—nothing but a miserable little five hundred dollar equity in a life insurance policy. You're worth more dead than alive."[26]

Bailey, taking Potter's words at face value, decides to jump from the bridge and drown himself in the town's river. His family can collect the life insurance money.

Bailey's despair echoes Scrooge's, but it is accompanied by

FIGURE 5.4. *It's a Wonderful Life*, 1946. Donna Reed and James Stewart. By permission of RKO/Photofest.

freshly fallen snow against the backdrop of an idealized American small town circa 1945. Still, Bailey's predicament represents the underside of the American Dream, a Norman Rockwell illustration dropped into a muddy pool of water. While George, unlike Scrooge, has family and friends, his dark night of the soul is an existential crisis that he must work through with a little help from Angel Clarence.

In George Bailey's crisis at the end of *It's a Wonderful Life,* he has been pushed to the edge, reaching the bottom rung of the seasonal blues ladder. His loneliness, despair, and repressed desire are pitiable any time of the year, though doubly against the backdrop of the Christmas season. While *It's a Wonderful Life* achieves a happy ending, the skeptic may wonder if Bailey, like his English counterpart Scrooge, will properly keep Christmas in the future. While Bailey has found resolution with the help of family and friends—a close-knit community in which he plays a vital role—he has only resolved his personal despair for Christmas of 1945. To expand on one critic's remarks on the movie, there is no guarantee—as *It's a Wonderful Life* comes to a close—that Bailey's anguish over earlier regrets will not reemerge during future Christmases. The holiday blues and hard times are always near, no more than one missed paycheck, one credit card bill, and one failed dream away.

Singing the Christmas Blues

Converting these conventional Christmas experiences—the blues and hard times—into popular song may have seemed like an unpromising task. Unlike a novella (*A Christmas Carol*) and movie (*It's a Wonderful Life*), a short lyric attached to a three-minute recording-studio performance left little room for development and an upturned ending. The lyrical form within American popular song was too compressed to focus on more than one emotion (happy *or* sad, nostalgic *or* melancholy), and often seemed better equipped to offer an impressionistic sketch than complex narrative. In "Christmas in Prison," that meant that Prine's persona never leaves jail and is never reunited with his true love, and that there is no happy ending. The listener never learns any concrete information about the narrator's life before prison, or what crime has placed him in prison. The ambiguity between the prisoner's dreams (to leave prison and be reunited with the one he loves) and their fulfillment is likewise left unresolved, leaving a melancholy residue. There is simply too little space and time within the popular song format to sketch a new scene or open a second chapter.

A melancholy mood attached itself to several kinds of Christmas lyrics, from songs about romantic difficulties to songs about hard times to songs about the holiday blahs. Even outside of Christmas music, the popular American song—whether country music, R&B, or mainstream pop—was no stranger to melancholy. Certain melancholy narratives, however, were much more familiar under the umbrella of popular music.

Songs about love gone wrong and romantic problems were probably as common as any within popular music. In 1943, Fred Astaire introduced "One for My Baby (And One More for the Road)," a song chronicling the end of a relationship. The lyric allows the downhearted narrator to repeat his sad affair to an anonymous bartender, with no attempt to offer hope (that the relationship might resume) or any silver lining. In the country weeper "I Can't Help It (If I'm Still in Love with You)," Hank Williams's persona relates a story of his lingering feelings for someone who has moved on to a new love. He is heartbroken when the song begins and when the song concludes. These songs were familiar within all genres of popular music during the 1940s and 1950s.

Songs about hard times, poverty, unemployment, and alcohol consumption were much less common within mainstream music. Even in the midst of the Depression, there were few mainstream songs that focused on hard times. One exception, Bing Crosby's version of "Brother, Can You Spare a Dime?" from 1934, was controversial; radio stations attempted to ban it.[27] Within country music, however, songs alluding to class and social values were more acceptable. In Tennessee Ernie Ford's "Sixteen Tons" (1955), the life of a coalminer is revealed to be one of relentless labor and low pay; in Kitty Wells's "I Heard the Jukebox Playing" (1952), a woman has been left at home to raise a baby while her husband spends his evenings in honky-tonks. In a similar way, Christmas songs centering on hard times offered a mixture of social realism mingled with conservative values.

Songs about the holiday blues are perhaps the most nebulous subcategory to properly define and pin down. It would be easy, in one sense, to trace the holiday blues to the blues themselves, a genre that offered a reflection of the mental and spiritual state of the lyric writer or singer. But complaints frequently touching on poverty, romantic difficulties, and sexual proclivities seemed unrelated to the holiday blues in the contemporary sense. Even while imprecise, the Christmas blahs show little concern with poverty, romance, or sex. Instead, someone suffering from the holiday blues was self-absorbed and dissatisfied in a nonspecific way.

In popular non-Christmas music, the Carpenters' "Rainy Days and Mondays" serves as an example of this tone, with the narrator talking in generalities—that nothing seems to fit and that she does not feel that she belongs. Karen Carpenter's persona also describes the mood as something that will pass as it has before. While this expression of melancholy does appear within everyday popular music, the idea seemed to work particularly well when married to seasonal complaints within the Christmas song.

"Blue Christmas" (1948)

> For those without families, Christmas is
> all too often a time of acute loneliness.
>
> Sheila Whiteley

COUNTRY AND WESTERN singer Doye O'Dell released one of the earliest versions of Billy Hayes and Jay W. Johnson's "Blue Christmas" in 1948, establishing the song—for the next eight years—as a country music standard. *Billboard* listed the recording under "Folk" and described O'Dell's "Blue Christmas" as a "Western-style Christmas ballad . . . warbled with blue feeling."[28] The publisher Choice Music, distributing the sheet music, offered nonmodestly that "Blue Christmas" was "the best Xmas song in the country."[29] Featuring prominent fiddle and steel guitar, along with cowboy-style harmony, "Blue Christmas" is delivered by O'Dell at a waltz pace, allowing the loneliness to sink in deep. O'Dell's persona has been left alone by the woman he loves, and while she will celebrate a white Christmas, his will be suffused in blue.

Ernest Tubb and the Texas Troubadours recorded "Blue Christmas" at a session in August of 1949 along with "White Christmas." Because of the latter song's popularity, "White Christmas" would be listed as the A-side; both songs, however, became hits (O'Dell's version of "Blue Christmas" did not). While Tubb's version of

"Blue Christmas" seemed to fit comfortably within the country music tradition, it departed musically from O'Dell's in one significant way.

There is no mistaking Tubb's recording as country, at least as the recording begins. His "foghorn" vocals are supported by a stripped-down country arrangement featuring prominent steel guitar. A guitar lead opens the song, followed by Tubb's vocal, and the setup promises a pure honky-tonk record. Approximately thirty seconds into the recording, however, Tubb is joined by the smooth singing of the Beasly Sisters. For fans of Tubb's untrained vocals (country music fans) and fans of Andrews Sisters–style vocals (pop music fans), the combination of two divergent styles might have seemed grating. From a musical standpoint, it is a cultural clash that never truly blends. Later, similar methods would be used to shape the Nashville Sound, offering a smoother-styled music that had the possibility of crossing beyond a country audience. If this was Tubb's aim, it seemed to work in spite of the clash: "Blue Christmas" appeared on the *Billboard* pop chart in 1949, rising to number 26.

"Blue Christmas" easily fell within the traditional heartbreak song category. Because Tubb's persona has less than three minutes to relate this sad tale, the listener never learns why the woman has left her husband (within the more conservative field of country music during the 1940s, it would be easy to assume that any couple who had lived together was married). We only know the narrator's point of view, and even then, we only learn of his heartbreak and loss. We sympathize with him (or, when a woman sings the song, with her) nonetheless because he expresses his lonesomeness in a direct manner that appears authentic: he is laying his heart out for the listener. Because he has been left alone during the Christmas

FIGURE 5.5. Russell Lee, "Unemployed Workers in Front of a Shack with Christmas Tree," 1938. Negative: nitrate; 35 mm. Library of Congress.

season, he may seem even more sympathetic to the listener (and the woman in the song less so even though we never meet her). If children had been left at home, as they have been in George Jones's "Lonely Christmas Call," the narrator would perhaps be even more sympathetic.

Tubb departed from O'Dell's original version in one other aspect, adding an extra verse to "Blue Christmas" (a verse that has seldom been used by other singers). The verse adds a religious element, asking the wife who has left him whether she will feel the same when she is praying on this Christmas as when the two of them prayed together in the past. The verse is obscure, and perhaps more than traditionally religious. It leaves the impression of judgment: perhaps, the singer seems to suggest, she has strayed from God in straying from her husband. The religious residue nonetheless remains, binding the song closer to country music tradition and the music's rural roots.

It is easy, in fact, to see "Blue Christmas" as the flipside of "White Christmas." While the narrator of "White Christmas" dreams of the perfect holiday, with children, presents, and snow, Tubb's narrator sees everything through a haze of blue. If he spends Christmas alone, the decorated tree means nothing; the snow that falls leads only to unhappy memories. If "White Christmas" is a song of homecoming, "Blue Christmas" is a song of a broken home; the singer cannot even dream of a happy homecoming or spiritual redemption because he is already at home without the hope of being joined by the one he loves for the holiday. Hope is replaced with sadness and longing.

"Blue Christmas" is also sad because there seems little chance of reconciliation in the future. In "Please Come Home for Christmas," Charles Brown's narrator remains hopeful of a happy reunion with the one he loves, despite the current romantic problems (or simply the distance between them); Tubb's narrator, however, seems fatalistically resolved to the separation. He never requests reconciliation, and when he describes the Christmas she will be celebrating as "white," it sounds like an accusation.

It would be easy to argue that "Blue Christmas" is simply a heartbreak song, barely dissimilar from Tubb's earlier hit, "Walking the Floor over You." Even the surface details of "Blue Christmas," however, point to a different conclusion. Heartbreak may be the underlying theme of "Blue Christmas" just as it is in Tubb's

"Walking the Floor over You," but heartbreak at Christmas is set against a backdrop of seasonal reminders and values. The Christmas tree, for instance, is something a husband and wife (or family) might decorate together; in separation, the decorated tree serves only as a painful reminder. Likewise, many of the traditional reasons for celebrating the holiday have been taken away. Christmas means gathering with friends and loved ones, singing carols, partaking in festive meals, and exchanging presents. Leaving a lover or husband behind, someone you have shared holy prayers with, inflicts a great emotional wound at Christmas. "Blue Christmas," then, is about more than heartbreak and a broken family: it is about defiling the sacredness of the holiday.

Later, when Elvis Presley recorded "Blue Christmas" in 1957, rock would transform the lyric from sad longing to a more aggressive, perhaps sexual, longing. In 1949, however, Tubb's version of "Blue Christmas" helped introduce an American audience to a new kind of holiday song, filled with heartbreak, accusations, and regret.

"Pretty Paper" (1963)

In 1963 pop singer Roy Orbison recorded and released "Pretty Paper," a Christmas single penned by Willie Nelson. *Billboard* wrote, "One of the best of the Christmas singles so far. It's a new song by Willie Nelson and it's given a power-packed, emotional reading by Orbison."[30] The song presented a simple juxtaposition between bright Christmas wrappings and an anonymous man on the street, between the laughter of Christmas cheer and the tears of a solitary man. The sympathetic qualities of "Pretty Paper" are buoyed by Orbison's plaintive, high-tone delivery. This is a lonely soloist singing about a lonely man in the midst of Christmas fellowship and joy.

Nelson sketched his lyric with broad brushstrokes. We learn nothing of the man's past (just as we learn nothing of the couple in "Blue Christmas"), of what has led him to beg or live on the street. In fact, Nelson never even states that the man *is* a beggar who lives on the street. If "Pretty Paper" is read literally, the man's wish—that the people who are passing by will stop and offer a Christmas greeting—may be no more than a desire for human contact and companionship (and not a desire for any kind of charity). Despite this vagueness, the lyric seems to require a response from the listener. Whether lonely or hungry, whether homeless or a beggar or temporarily down on his luck, the man is pitiable: Christmas is a time when everyone should be with friends and exchange sentiments with loved ones.

While "Pretty Paper" shares a number of qualities with "Blue Christmas" (notably loneliness), the song pushes beyond the concerns of romantic disappointment into the social arena. While Tubb's persona reproaches one person (his wife) for leaving him at the most family-centered time of year, Nelson's lyric lightly reproaches everyone who passes by the man on the street. Drawing from the same rural tradition that informed country music, the message of "Pretty Paper" is Christian-derived, though broadly so; Nelson's empathy could just as easily be described as humanistic. Christian or humanistic, Nelson nonetheless retains his country music influences by touching upon issues of class and the harshness of life in the city. While the happy shoppers who can afford nice Christmas presents never seem mean-spirited in "Pretty Paper" (they are in no way made to resemble Scrooge), they are nonetheless—in passing the man by—lacking in the true spirit of Christmas.

Although the moral of "Pretty Paper" is fairly easy to understand, the structure of the song is more complicated than "Blue Christmas." The recriminations of "Blue Christmas" are delivered in the form of a personal letter, with the writer expressing his sorrow and disappointment to the one who has left him behind. The layering of "Pretty Paper," on the other hand, has more in common with Henry James than Hank Williams. The song's narration switches between omniscient (a street scene at Christmas) and second person (the feelings of one man within that street scene as imagined by the song's narrator). Nelson's narrator paints the first scene broadly, the second with a handful of intimate details; the first reveals the festive Christmas atmosphere of any city, the latter the feelings and experience of one man. Unlike many first-person songs ("White Christmas," "Blue Christmas") in which the listener often conflates the narrator with the singer (i.e., Bing Crosby is relating his own feelings about Christmas), the more distant and partially omniscient observations in "Pretty Paper" emanate from an outside observer.

One narrative sleight of hand also ties both sections of the song together. Comparing the laughter in the street to the sadness of the man, one stanza ends with "cries." Following this, the song returns to the chorus's pretty paper and ribbons, potentially leaving the impression that the man on the street is crying out and bemoaning the pretty paper and beautiful sentiments of Christmas. He both "cries" and "cries out."

The social outsider in "Pretty Paper" shares qualities with the two protagonists of the 1945 Christmas movie, *I'll Be Seeing You*. Over the course of two hours, *I'll Be Seeing You* manages to provide a Hollywood ending for Joseph Cotten (Sergeant Zachary Morgan) and Ginger Rogers (Mary Marshall), though the mood that dominates the film and the residue that remains is darkly tinted. Released in 1945 as World War II came to a close, the movie features two narratives wrapped around the secrets of the two main characters. One character (Mary Marshall) has received a prison pass, allowing her to visit her uncle and aunt (her parents are dead) in the town of Pine Hill during the holiday, while the other is a shell-shocked soldier (Zachary Morgan) on leave to regain his psychological balance. While the movie viewer is invited to sympathize with both characters—Mary Marshall is serving the remainder of a sentence for manslaughter while Zachary Morgan is suffering from posttraumatic syndrome related to an experience in the war—it is also clear that each experience sets them apart from the average person and outside the community of Pine Hill.

Because of these secrets and the accompanying social baggage, both Mary and Zachary seem unable to enter into the mainstream of American life; the holiday dinner and fellowship freely given by Aunt Clara and Uncle Henry offers the promise of normal life but also emphasizes Marshall's and Morgan's distance from it. Even marrying and starting a new life, an important component of the American Dream, seems an impossible hope for a woman with a prison record and a man suffering from mental trauma. In a scene in the family kitchen, Mary speaks of her dreams with Aunt Clara:

> MARY MARSHALL: Coming out into the world and . . . even coming here, I had a feeling that . . .
>
> MRS. MARSHALL: Honey, you've got to stop being afraid. You've got to stop feeling that you're branded like people were

in the old days. You've done something. You're paying your debt to society. Most people are willing to let it go at that.

MARY MARSHALL: I know, Aunt Sarah, but coming out into the world and seeing everybody in uniform, everybody doing something . . . I just don't belong. I don't fit in. And dreams that I've had for the future are just impossible.

MRS. MARSHALL: Well, most dreams are, Mary. It's just the dreaming that counts. Nobody gets exactly what he wants out of life. One of the first things you learn is to make compromises with your dreams.

MARY MARSHALL: But I'm not talking about palaces and rainbows, Aunt Sarah. I'm talking about a home. A home like this with a kitchen and a stove and an icebox, and a husband, and a child.[31]

While likable, warm people, both Morgan and Marshall seem trapped within the social limitations of America in the mid-1940s; because of his war experience (during a time when these psychological disorders were less understood and perhaps seen as less sympathetic), he may be considered less of a man, and because of her manslaughter sentence (accidentally pushing her boss out of a window when he made unwanted advances), she may be considered a tainted woman. In the town of Pine Hill where Uncle Henry and Aunt Clara live, both Morgan and Marshall would be forever labeled.

Nelson's sketch in "Pretty Paper" renders another lost soul as a broad symbol for any American on the outside looking in; for any person who, for any reason, has been excluded from family, friends, material goods, and Christmas gaiety. As a broad representative, he serves to remind the busy people in "Pretty Paper," along with everyone who listens to the song, that there are those who have very little for Christmas (emotionally, materially, and spiritually), and that there are people who are unable to afford exchanging pretty sentiments on pretty paper. He is alone, perhaps hungry, and seems destined to remain on the street throughout Christmas. While everyone passing him by may be accepted within society as materially prosperous, they are nonetheless impoverished by the man on the street's presence. Still, there seems no way to close the gap—to stop, to invite him home, or just to totally ignore him. Loneliness and regret are left hanging in the air as "Pretty Paper" closes, tingeing an otherwise festive occasion. In this symbolic role, the man on the street is similar to a ghost in Dickens's *A Christmas Carol,* revealing another side of American life and pricking the conscience of all those who witness it.

As a pop song, "Pretty Paper" may have seemed unusual and unusually depressing during the Christmas season of 1963. It is interesting to speculate—because of the unusual subject matter of "Pretty Paper"—about the song's reception in the winter of 1963 within the United States. On November 9, *Billboard* noted, "Release is imminent of Roy Orbison's British-recorded 'Pretty Paper.'"[32] By the time "Pretty Paper" had debuted on the *Billboard's* Adult Contemporary and Hot charts on December 14, however, the pulse and temper of American life had been radically altered. During the Christmas season of 1963, Americans were absorbing the shock and mourning the assassination of President John F. Kennedy (in Dallas on November 22). Addressing the Congress a week after the shooting, President Johnson evoked the moment. "The greatest leader of our time has been struck down by the foulest deed of our time. Today John Fitzgerald Kennedy lives on in the immortal words and works that he left behind. He lives on in the mind and memories of mankind. He lives on in the hearts of his countrymen."[33]

While "Pretty Paper" was perhaps an unusual song to become popular, it seems to have matched the mood of the American people during a difficult moment.

FIGURE 5.6. "Extended Family Gathers at the Mantel on Christmas Day at the Residence of C. Michael Paul in Palm Beach, Florida," 1962. Negative. John F. Kennedy Library.

"Christmas Time Is Here" (1965)

While psychologists had been writing about the Christmas blues since the 1940s, popular American culture "discovered" the syndrome in the 1960s. "Christmas in the 1960s," writes Elizabeth Pleck, "was a special time of year to feel alienated. Rather than being simply a convenient expression for collective anguish in a deeply troubled, conflict-ridden decade, the term 'alienation' was frequently invoked in relation to America's single most important holiday."[34] As the optimism of the 1960s gave way to youth rebellion, assassination, and war, the Christmas song itself temporarily seemed at odds with the cultural moment. While pop musicians of the 1950s had seemed happy to make the obligatory Christmas album, rock musicians after the Beatles (at the beginning of 1964 in the United States) mostly ignored Christmas music. Despite the perceived shortcomings the American Christmas song had accrued by 1965 (that it was nonserious, children's music), one holiday album pushed beyond nostalgia and Santa Claus to capture the zeitgeist of an evolving era.

One of the perennial products of American popular culture during the 1960s (and beyond) was *A Charlie Brown Christmas* from 1965, a thirty-minute (with commercials) animated cartoon based on the Charles M. Shultz comic strip. Whether considering the cartoon or the accompanying soundtrack (with the same name), the listener finds that Christmas loneliness ("Blue Christmas") and charitable impulses ("Pretty Paper") have been replaced with a broader phenomenon: a bad case of the holiday blues. Whereas Ernest Tubb may have bemoaned his missing sweetheart and Willie Nelson lamented hard times for outsiders, Charlie Brown expressed a general melancholy and dissatisfaction

FIGURE 5.7. *A Charlie Brown Christmas*, 1965. By permission of CBS/Photofest.

against the backdrop of the Vince Guaraldi Trio soundtrack. As Peanuts' creator Shultz noted: "More and more, Christmas is set up for us as a day that is going to be so joyful. And somehow we don't seem to be able to reach the joy we're told we're supposed to have. We just are not magazine models smiling in front of a tree—real life isn't that way."[35] Either Christmas no longer held its traditional meaning, or those suffering from Dickens's syndrome seemed unable to find it. As a result, Charlie Brown's attempt to explain what was missing from the modern holiday only produces a laundry list of familiar complaints: loneliness, commercialism, and pink aluminum trees. Whatever the cause, he is left with the feeling that something has been lost; he longs for a different kind of Christmas experience (more traditional, more meaningful), but he has no idea how to create one.

"Christmas Time Is Here," an original song from *A Charlie Brown Christmas* soundtrack, aptly replicates the holiday blues in sound. Reading the words on the lyric sheet is deceptive: "Christmas Time Is Here" appears to be a joyful ode to the winter season. The lyric describes the cheerful emotions experienced by children at Christmas, and the song's use of common holiday symbols—yuletide, sleigh bells, and snowflakes—resembles a pared-down version of "The Christmas Song" for kids. The performance, however, like most of the material on the soundtrack, creates a bluer mood, descending from nostalgia to melancholy. A group of children perform the song at a lethargic pace, as though they were sleepwalking through a winter wonderland. The melancholy vocal and cadence take precedence over the uplifting lyric, suffusing the world of the Peanuts gang in a thick holiday gloom.

In one scene from *A Charlie Brown Christmas,* Lucy, masquerading as a psychologist, consults with Charlie Brown. If the cartoon had been made during the middle of the 1980s instead of the 1960s, Lucy might have diagnosed Charlie Brown with seasonal affective disorder (SAD). While the seasonal disorder included a number of symptoms, it was most often identified with the lack of sunlight during the winter months. All Charlie Brown would have really needed to recapture the spirit of Christmas, then, was more sunlight.

Norman E. Rosenthal, however, argues in *Winter Blues* that SAD and the holiday blues are really two separate phenomena.

> The common element of sadness between SAD and the holiday blues is where the resemblance between these two conditions usually stops. When we refer to "depression" as a clinical term . . . we think of a sustained state lasting several weeks that is accompanied by physical changes—for example, in eating, sleeping, energy level, and daily functioning. There is no evidence that most people reacting to Christmas or the holidays exhibit this picture, whereas it is typical for SAD patients to show all of these features.[36]

Lucy might have better diagnosed Charlie Brown's condition, then, as seasonal melancholy.

On the surface, songs like "Christmas Time Is Here" may seem self-indulgent, similar perhaps to the self-indulgence of the holiday blues itself. Unlike true depression, the person suffering from the holiday blues is merely feeling sorry for him- or herself. This negative interpretation of the music and Charlie Brown's condition, however, overlooks the zeitgeist that undergirded the seasonal melancholy for many Americans during the 1960s and beyond. More than capturing the sound of the holiday blues, "Christmas Time Is Here" also revealed a feeling that lay just beneath the surface of Christmas songs focusing on loss, loneliness, and want. This feeling politely suggested that something about the modern holiday was broken or missing, that there was a disconnect between Christmas present and past. While the individual—like Charlie Brown—may experience this feeling, this sense of loss, it also resonated within the broader American culture.

The viewer may feel that he or she has been fooled at the end of *A Charlie Brown Christmas,* just as viewers may react to the happy ending pasted onto *It's a Wonderful Life*. Even if Charlie Brown has learned the true meaning of Christmas as the cartoon seems to suggest, melancholy continues to linger like the fading notes of the soundtrack. He seems no happier in *It's the Great Pumpkin, Charlie Brown* a year later (though the major emphasis may be more firmly focused on Linus's spiritual crisis), receiving rocks instead of candy while trick-or-treating. Brown seems likely to remain the eternal good-time loser, wrapped in a veneer of American naiveté that is only one football kick away from landing him on his backside. As Brown himself summarizes his own holiday blues at the beginning of *A Charlie Brown Christmas,* "I almost wish there weren't a holiday season. I know nobody likes me. Why do we have to have a holiday season to emphasize it?"[37]

The Limits of Sympathy

Even considered from the vantage point of thirty years later, Tom Waits's "Christmas Card from a Hooker in Minneapolis" is both unusual and depressing as holiday fare. Waits, with his rough vocal style cataloging the down-and-outs of the city streets, probably seemed as unlikely a candidate to deliver a Christmas song as John Prine. "Christmas Card from a Hooker in Minneapolis," however, was typical of Waits's other material from the 1970s and also typical of how far the Christmas song had fallen from the idealism of "White Christmas." Waits simply wrote and performed a Christmas song about one of his down-and-out characters.

As one might expect from the title alone, "Christmas Card from a Hooker in Minneapolis" pushes beyond even the depressing themes of "Blue Christmas," "Pretty Paper," and "Christmas Time Is Here." Performed in a loose jazz style, almost "talked-out" more than sung, the lyric's long narrative and over four-minute length also challenges the listener. In the song, a hooker references pregnancy, a dirty bookstore, drugs, alcohol, and prison. While she attempts to offer her own version of a happy holiday, explaining that she is clean of drugs and booze, married to a trombone player, and expecting a baby, she is really—she finally confesses—in prison and needs to borrow money. The lyric holds true to its title: the entire story is from the woman's point of view, leaving the listener to guess what the recipient of the postcard (Charlie) might think or how he might respond. A happy ending, however, seems unlikely. Whereas it might be easy to imagine the narrator of "Blue Christmas" eventually meeting someone new (or that his wife may eventually return) or the children in "Christmas Time Is Here" growing into less melancholy adults, "Christmas Card from a Hooker in Minneapolis" seems to hold little hope for any kind of happy future. "Christmas Card from a Hooker in Minneapolis" is an American portrait from the bottom of the barrel.

When considering broader social criticism and the Christmas song, it is worth noting that while some commentators have labeled Dickens's *Carol*'s philosophy as radical, the most damning portraits within *A Christmas Carol* are those of the poor. Indeed, the only extended description of the poor in *A Christmas Carol* focuses on a handful of lowlifes who bargain for the deceased Scrooge's clothes and bed curtains within the vision presented by the Ghost of Christmas Future. This rough and tumble lot are crude figures without ethical qualms. Referring to a shirt removed from Scrooge, the woman selling it says: "'Putting it on him to be buried in, to be sure,' replied the woman with a laugh. 'Somebody was fool enough to do it, but I took it off again. If calico an't good enough for such a purpose, it isn't good enough for anything. It's quite as becoming to the body. He can't look uglier than he did in that one.'"[38]

Although Scrooge may be a penny pincher who shows no mercy with a debtor's late payments, he never does anything illegal. The entire bartering ritual enacted by this scrappy crew is portrayed as unseemly, with Dickens offering an inside view of the London black market where sport is made of a dead man's misfortune. These lower-class folks are not sympathetic, and while they may seem every bit as reprehensible as Scrooge, if not more so, they are never visited by Christmas ghosts. Scrooge, the middle-class financier, is redeemed, whereas Dickens seems unconcerned about these meager figures.

In *The Battle for Christmas,* Stephen Nissenbaum provides a better understanding of why *A Christmas Carol* was successful in America. While *A Christmas Carol* has been interpreted as a radical strike against industrialization and nineteenth-century capitalism, the actual targets of Dickens's slim book are much more modest. Within the book, Dickens never calls for the dismantling of industrialism or the capitalist system that supported it. There is never a hint that the social carnage of Ignorance and Want, the two children tucked in the wings of the Ghost of Christmas Present, has been caused by reckless industrialism. Instead, Dickens suggests a more modest way of addressing the dispossessed within industrial cities: charity. Anyone who has done well monetarily should donate to charitable organizations because these institutions serve as negotiators between the middle class and the urban poor. "Charity allows us to congratulate ourselves on the fact that we give," notes John Storey. "And charity certainly relieves suffering but what it does not do is change the causes of suffering."[39] These institutions help the poor, but they also help maintain social order.

Christmas songs like "Blue Christmas," "Pretty Paper," and "Christmas Time Is Here" worked within the framework built by Dickens and American apostles like Frank Capra. A broken romance can be sad but never maudlin; a man can face loneliness and hard times but never true hunger or deprivation; and sincere types can question the meaning of Christmas but never suggest that the celebration is meaningless.

Christmas songs focusing on the blues and hard times, then, attempted a delicate balance. It was okay to recognize that the Christmas holiday was difficult for many people, but reconciliation and hope must remain. A separated lover may return on

FIGURE 5.8. *Scrooge*, 1951. Louise Hampton, Ernest Thesiger, Kathleen Harrison, and Miles Malleson. By permission of United Artists/Photofest.

Christmas Eve; a shopper may stop and offer comfort to the man on the street; and a lonely boy may discover, through the help of a friend, the true meaning of Christmas. But there can be no extended depression or threat of suicide; the blues must be allowed to pass as they naturally should. Any American who falls outside this carefully balanced paradigm risks becoming an outcast or marginalized, unreconciled to the national holiday experience. Americans are allowed to struggle with the blues, Dickens's syndrome, or post-traumatic holiday syndrome, but they must have Christmas.

A VISIT FROM SAINT NICHOLAS.

BY CLEMENT C. MOORE.

'Twas the night before Christmas, when all thro' the house,

Not a creature was stirring, not even a mouse;
The stockings were hung by the chimney with care,
In hopes that St. Nicholas soon would be there;

2

The children were nestled all snug in their beds
While visions of sugar-plums danced through their heads:
And mamma in her 'kerchief, and I in my cap,
Had settled our brains for a long winter's nap,

FIGURE 6.1. "Visit of Saint Nicholas," ca. 1850. General Collection, Beinecke Rare Book and Manuscript Library, Yale University.

6

Satire: Surviving Christmas

The
celebration of
Christmas as decreed by Clement
Clarke Moore, Charles Dickens, Norman
Rockwell (and the Coca-Cola company) and Walt
Disney Enterprises is for many a tyrannical regime,
emphasizing the shortfall of their own family lives (or
lack thereof). Despite the good cheer around the Cratchit
table, this fantasy Christmas is available only to those
who have the money (and the room) for a full-sized
tree and a turkey dinner for the whole family.

Kim Newman

Hail, Satire!
Hail, clear-eyed, sharp-tongued,
hot-tempered, outwardly disillusioned and
secretly idealistic Muse! Mother of comedy, sister of
Tragedy, defender and critic of Philosophy, hail! You are
a difficult companion, a mistress sometimes elusive and
tantalizing, sometimes harsh and repellent; but in
your mercurial presence no one is ever bored.

Gilbert Highet, *The Anatomy of Satire*

IN THE first eight lines of "A Visit from St. Nicholas" (1823) Clement C. Moore gives the reader a picture of domestic tranquility:

'Twas the night before Christmas, when all through the house
Not a creature was stirring, not even a mouse;
The stockings were hung by the chimney with care,
In hopes that St. Nicholas soon would be there;
The children were nestled all snug in their beds,
While visions of sugar-plums danced in their heads;
And Mamma in her 'kerchief, and I in my cap,
Had just settled our brains[1] for a long winter's nap[2]

These lines offer a key to understanding the remainder of the poem, even though the reader has yet to reach the stated subject: "A Visit from St. Nicholas." The preamble, however, has framed the visit carefully: it will take place against the backdrop of a middle-class home and family. As imagined by the emerging American middle class during the 1820s and beyond, St. Nicholas would become an essential part of the domestic Christmas with children—snug in their beds and dreaming of sweets—placed squarely at the center.

Perhaps surprisingly, the children that dream of sugar plums never make another appearance in "A Visit from St. Nicholas." Children do make an extended appearance in another poem penned around 1856, some twenty-three years after Moore's had been published. Instead of following within the tradition that Moore had outlined in "A Visit from St. Nicholas," however, the anonymous author took the low road; instead of building on the traditions sketched by Moore, the anonymous author lampooned them. "The Night After Christmas" would become one of the first parodies of Moore's poem, exchanging domestic serenity for the aftermath of too much Christmas dinner and too many sweets. In exchange for innocent children nestled snug in their beds and dreaming of sweets, the reader would be assaulted by grossly ill urchins revealing—literally—everything they had (over)eaten.

The first eight lines of "The Night After Christmas" mimicked the domestic quietude of the original, while also suggesting that all was not quite right:

> 'Twas the night after Christmas, when all through the house,
> Every soul was abed, and still as a mouse,
> The stockings so lately St. Nicholas' care,
> Were emptied of all that was eatable there,
> The darlings had been duly tucked in their beds—
> With very full stomachs and pains in their heads.
> I was dozing away in my new cotton cap,
> And Nancy was rather far gone in a nap[3]

When the clatter arises in "The Night After Christmas," however, it has nothing to do with the arrival of Santa Claus (it is the night *after* Christmas). Instead, the noise emanates from pale-faced children who are suffering the aftermath of holiday excess. The author proceeds to list all of the items that have been rejected by the children's stomachs. "Now Turkey, now Stuffing, Plum Pudding of course, / Now Custards and Crullers, and Cranberry Sauce, / Before outraged nature all went to the wall, / Yes—Lollypops, Flapdoodle, dinner and all."[4] After the husband attempts to resolve the crisis with Ipecac, the wife suggests calling the doctor, who arrives—like Santa in "A Visit from St. Nicholas"—"with a bound." While the doctor saves the day—dosing the children to rid them of the remaining contents of their stomachs—he seems to be drunk ("His cheeks looked like *Port* and his breath smelt of *Sherry*").[5] Clearly "The Night After Christmas" undercuts all middle-class pretensions without mercy.

By the time the doctor shouts, "They'll be well to-morrow—good night! Jones—good night," Moore's sugar-plum dream of middle-class children has been transformed into an unpleasant hallucination.[6] Sleeping cherubs, a quiet house, and a tidy peddler have been bartered for retching, heaving children and a doctor on a bender (he has not "shaved for a fortnight or more").[7] In the hands of a clever scribbler, "A Night Before Christmas" has become "The Nightmare After Christmas."

For many readers, it was perhaps easy to accept "The Night After Christmas" as a light parody, a cunning take-off that attempted little more than to have fun at the original's expense. As Moore's poem grew in fame, it practically invited others to deflate it. Even as the middle class placed children at the center of an American Christmas, many would have related to the tendency of kids to overdo it during the holiday. And even if the anonymous author wished to convey something more serious (that kids were spoiled during the holidays, for instance), surely the poem still worked on a nonsensical level. Crude, perhaps, but silly-fun nonetheless.

"Let me say without hesitation," writes Martin Gardner in his introduction to *The Annotated Night Before Christmas* where "The Night After Christmas" is reprinted, "that I consider most of the parodies in this book doggerel, or close to doggerel, whereas Moore's original ballad, which started it all, is an example of popular verse at its best."[8] A parody or travesty, then, was a bad copy of an average product, primarily designed for an easy laugh at the expense of the original.

Other readers, however, may have realized that "The Night After Christmas" also served as a biting critique of the original. By the end of "The Night After Christmas," the middle-class world that had wished to center Christmas on Santa Claus and children had turned into an outlandish nightmare. In the satirist's hands, elements that had been stamped by the middle class as sacred (both within and outside of Christmas)—a holiday dinner with traditional dishes, children's treats, Santa Claus, and even the family doctor—became sullied over the course of the poem. Instead of a respectable, ordered home as in "A Visit from St. Nicholas," the reader is left with a topsy-turvy household and children as gluttons, either unwilling to mind parents or, worse still, undisciplined by parents. "The Night After Christmas" was a poem for which no one wanted illustrations.

When the Christmas song emerged during the 1940s, it was likewise only a matter of time before songwriters created parodies, satires, and light-comic lyrics that mimicked and inverted holiday traditions. Most of these songs were designated as children's songs and categorized as "novelty." Songs like "I Saw Mommy Kissing Santa Claus" (1952), "Nuttin' for Christmas" (1955), and "The Chipmunk Song" (1958) were mostly enjoyable nonsense, focusing on Christmas from a child's point of view. "Novelty songs have established a special niche in holiday music that has been extremely lucrative," writes Steve Otfinoski, "ever since Spike Jones's unleashed 'All I Want for Christmas Is My Two Front Teeth' on the world and Gene Autry warbled 'Rudolph the Red-Nosed Reindeer.'"[9]

On occasion, however, children's novelty songs dipped into a more critical or sardonic mode, such as the familiar version of "All I Want for Christmas (Is My Two Front Teeth)" (1948) by Spike Jones and His City Slickers. Unlike the smoother version of the song by Nat King Cole, singer George Rock delivered a vocal lisp that—to some listeners—rendered the young boy of the song more irritating than enduring. In this way, Otfinoski notes in *The Golden Age of Novelty Songs,* Jones and His City Slickers undercut the "holiday sentimentality" of cute children singing Christmas songs.[10] The vocal lisp also added an air of skepticism that questioned the seemingly straightforward meaning of the lyric: no child wanted to forgo all Christmas presents in exchange for his or her two front teeth. Another example can be taken from Stan Freberg's "Nuttin' for Christmas." At the end of the song, after a young boy has delivered the song's moral (you better be good if you want Christmas gifts from Santa), he collaborates with a thief to steal his family's silverware. Both songs suggested that while many children may be snuggly asleep and dreaming of sugar plums, others were up to no good.

Most comic songs for adults, like most novelty songs for children, were similarly light-hearted in approach. Mabel Scott's "Boogie Woogie Santa Claus" (1948) pictured a modern Santa, hip to the latest dance trends. Eartha Kitt's "Santa Baby" (1953) balanced the carnivalesque with a healthy dose of materialism: if the lyric seemed risqué for the time period, it nonetheless embraced the status quo of the American consumer. Basically, "Boogie Woogie Santa Claus" and "Santa Baby" were novelty songs for adults, or at least they were consumed as such.

Sometimes, however, satirical songs drew from a more critical tradition calling into question the common—and sometimes sacred—myths and ideas surrounding the holiday. Familiar Christmas material—"A Visit from St. Nicholas," *A Christmas Carol,* "Jingle Bells," "Yes, Virginia," Currier and Ives, and "The Gift of the Magi"—was fair game, serving as a shortcut to satire and parody. Americans knew these stories, illustrations, and songs as well as they knew "America the Beautiful" and the Pledge of Allegiance, so they knew right away when something had been changed. Recognizing the variation, in fact, was part of the fun. When a songwriter wished to satirize Christmas heritage, borrowing the melody of "Jingle Bells" gave him an easy "in," even if the lyric had nothing to do with the original; using story elements from *A Christmas Carol* (as with Stan Freberg's "Green Chritma" in 1958) assured that most listeners would be familiar with the setup, even if it was given a new twist.

Unlike the light comedy of novelty, however, satire's twist was a critical one, taking beloved myths—from the image of a benevolent Santa Claus to faith in the institution of family to the vision of local and regional communities—and inverting them or discarding them altogether. More than a childish put-on, satire dared suggest that an American Christmas was often less than the culture advertised, and perhaps not worth the trouble.

As one might imagine, any satirical song that critiqued favored Christmas customs was always at risk of offending the listener. Humor, however, allowed the satirist to cut deeper into the American fabric than would have been allowed otherwise. Because the meaning of satire and parody was often ambiguous, they also allowed the listener (and the songwriter) to have it both ways: at once "The Night After Christmas" appeared as a light-hearted lampoon and a sharp-barbed parody, either stimulating innocent laughter or undercutting the sacred hush of Moore's poem.

Even so, few satirical Christmas songs reached the status of classics. The occasional satire—Yogi Yorgesson's "I Yust Go Nuts at Christmas" (1949), Stan Freberg's "Green Chritma," and Tom Lehrer's "A Christmas Carol" (1959)—either appeared briefly on the charts and disappeared or became underground favorites (all of these songs would later be issued on *Dr. Demento Presents: Greatest Christmas Novelty* in 1989). Others continued to be recycled against a backdrop of variations on "The Twelve Days of Christmas," such as Allen Sherman's "The Twelve Gifts of Christmas" (1963) and Bob and Doug McKenzie's version of "The Twelve Days of Christmas" (1981). Although there were exceptions, earlier holiday satires (through 1963) seem to have been more acceptable to a broader audience, partly because they most often attacked everybody's favorite target: commercialism.

After 1963, songs like the Sonics' "Don't Believe in Christmas" (1965) filtered holiday traditions through a heavier mesh of cynicism, perhaps limiting commercial appeal. Still, even the oddest Christmas songs continued to chart. In 1972 Commander Cody reached number seventeen on *Billboard*'s Christmas chart with "Daddy's Drinking Up Our Christmas," a song as easy to interpret as straight country music than as satire. Likewise, Elmo and Patsy's "Grandma Got Run Over by a Reindeer" segued from *Billboard*'s Christmas chart in 1983 (number two) to the Country chart in 1984 (also number two). Even if in less demand than nostalgic and romantic material, satirical Christmas songs worked like an undercurrent to mainstream culture, questioning familiar holiday rituals that most Americans seemed willing to accept without too much reflection.

The Serious Business of Satire

Christmas novelty songs have generally fallen into two categories—good and bad. The "good" songs, like "Rudolph," are often aimed at the children in us and celebrate the holiday with heart-warming humor and fantasy. The "bad" songs, by their very irreverence, undermine modern Christmas's emotional and material excesses. While the latter has often had the more satisfying and lasting impact, it is the former that has usually sold more records.

Steve Otfinoski, *The Golden Age of Novelty Songs*

IT WOULD be easy to confuse satirical and carnival Christmas songs, since both seem to invert and subvert holiday traditions. Likewise, it would be easy for the carnival song to include traces of satire and for the satirical song to include elements of carnival. These crossovers and confusions, however, rest only on the surface, serving mostly as distractions. The main dividing line between carnival and satire is one of purpose: carnival wishes for little more than sensuous pleasure and a good time, while satire—beneath the laughter—demands a more serious appraisal.

The carnival song may offend the mainstream values of the average American, but it seldom sets out to change or challenge those values directly. Carnival *may* challenge tradition nonetheless, but that is not usually its purpose: it simply desires to go its own way and do its own thing. Carnival even accepts that most of the time, its practices are objectionable. During festivals and holidays, however, carnival allows for a brief break from mainstream mores and customs, offering an outlet for behavior that would seem outlandish any other time. By serving as no more than a respite, and by expressing little interest in reform, carnival—standing as the opposite of what is considered the "norm"—could even be viewed as reinforcing middle class ideas on the proper way to celebrate Christmas.

Satire, on the other hand, has Christmas squarely in its sights. Beneath the humor, satire is serious business or at least seriously offensive, either offering a social critique aimed at improving a given situation or simply attempting to deflate, level, and undermine something it finds hypocritical. As Gilbert Highet notes in *The Anatomy of Satire,* satire is of two minds:

> There are . . . two main conceptions of the purpose of satire, and two different types of satirist. One likes most people, but thinks they are rather blind and foolish. He tells the truth with a smile, so that he will not repel them but cure them of that ignorance which is their worst fault. . . . The other type hates most people, or despises them. He believes rascality is triumphant in his world; or he says . . . that though he loves individuals he detests mankind. His aim therefore is not to cure, but to wound, to punish, to destroy.[11]

One satirist wishes for nothing more than to reform Christmas; another wishes for nothing less than to eradicate it.

It may seem surprising that critical satire—even with its humorous spoonful of sugar—has ever been tolerated, especially in relation to a holiday with as many sacred connotations as Christmas (from the Holy family to the American family). Any song, after all, had to be deemed as nonoffensive to the majority of listeners to be considered commercially viable by a recording label. In general, popular music (and popular culture) was more concerned with reflecting public taste than offending it. Christmas songs, however, drew from a critical tradition that had been enfolded into the rites of the holiday. *A Christmas Carol,* for instance, was basically a morality play about the proper way to celebrate the Yuletide (though without humor); similar lessons could be found in the "Yes, Virginia" letter, "The Gift of the Magi," and many Christmas-themed movies (including *It's a Wonderful Life*). It was okay to preach about celebrating Christmas in the right spirit, and

FIGURE 6.2. Will Crawford, "Hands Up!," 1912. Photomechanical print: offset, color. Library of Congress.

likewise acceptable to criticize those who failed to do so. During the 1940s and 1950s, most Christmas song satires followed within the Dickens tradition.

In the introduction to a live recording of Tom Lehrer's "A Christmas Carol," he tells his audience that most of the holiday songs heard on the radio failed to reflect what Americans cherished most deeply: money. His new Christmas song, he says, will correct that oversight. In the song, Lehrer offers a series of clever observations, challenging familiar holiday truisms. If everyone appears more open-handed and friendly during the Christmas season, it only emphasizes the money-grubbing of the remainder of the year; likewise, the sincerity of a gift exchange becomes questionable when the receiver expresses a greater concern with a gift's monetary value than the sentiment behind it. While Lehrer may be satirizing both capitalism and the average American who buys into it, most of his barbs are easily deflected: it is easy to agree with the perennial complaint that Christmas is (or is in danger of becoming) too commercial. No one, however, has to apply Lehrer's criticism personally.

In the end, it is easy to see Lehrer and other satirists as preaching to the choir. The foundation for an American Christmas was solid; the problem was the way that merchants and individuals kept the holiday. Nothing was wrong with gift-giving per se; some folks just tended to overdo it. Reforming Christmas, then, simply meant returning it to its purer, less commercial origins.

Stan Freberg's "Merry Chritma" drama adapted *A Christmas Carol* to a modern American setting, with a greedy businessman—wishing to exploit the holiday—standing in for Dickens's Scrooge. Once again, the criticisms may seem harsh, but only out of the context of the critical tradition that had been built around

Christmas. Historian Mark Connelly makes a similar observation about critiques within popular holiday movies. "The Santa Claus movies all make reference to the nature of a capitalistic society. A critique of that society is always included but it is also always a highly contained and tightly regulated critique."[12] Within this tradition, these satires lose much of their bite, offering a conservative corrective with which most people could generally agree.

Critical satire, however, also had a ruder cousin with bad table manners. Often, even these satires would be tempered to the limits of public taste: it was okay to suggest many things, as long as no one was supposed to take them seriously. It was okay to have daddy kissing Santa Claus (in the 1980s), as long as mommy removed the Santa suit at the end of the song.

Even within the bounds of public taste, however, satirical songs like Yorgi Yorgesson's "Yingle Bells" (1949) and "I Yust Go Nuts at Christmas" (1949) left a lingering aftertaste that allowed the listener to look at the less attractive side of Yuletide fun. There was no attempt to reform Christmas, to turn the clock back and make the celebration like it used to be—there was only a comical effort to send up familiar holiday complaints such as hangovers, loud children, and relatives. These were things that one had to laugh at, probably because there was no way to fix them. Others like "Grandma Got Run Over by a Reindeer" (1979) served as nothing less than a travesty of everything that the mainstream American Christmas had represented. Whether you laughed or turned off the radio depended on the listener.

Following the 1960s and 1970s, when Christmas seemed to lose its prestige as a communal American celebration, the satirical holiday song adopted a sharper and more offensive edge. And while many performers recorded Christmas singles during the 1980s and beyond for commercial reasons, others simply recorded them because they had something to express about the holiday (even if it meant reaching no more than a small or underground audience). As Christmas audiences fragmented, it also became easier for a satirical song to remain critical while no longer conforming to broadly shared cultural norms. Weird Al Yankovic may have fallen within the reformist tradition with "Christmas at Ground Zero" (1986), but it is doubtful that the majority of Americans believed that it was funny to wipe out all holiday culture—no matter how degraded—with nuclear weapons.

Even with the nonsatirical comic song in the 1980s, the broader American culture seemed more willing to accept material that would have been considered offensive in the past. In 1987, comedian Bob Rivers turned the most sacred of all American Christmas songs, "White Christmas," into the country-bumpkin "White Trash Christmas." While many may have considered this sacrilege, Rivers's *Twisted Christmas* (1987) nonetheless showed up on *Billboard*'s Christmas chart in 1988. A Christmas song no longer needed to please everyone.

"Yingle Bells" and "I Yust Go Nuts at Christmas" (1949)

> Christmas carols have also been popular targets of novelty artists. They have had great fun in setting these age-old melodies of Christmas past to contemporary lyrics that skewer the rampant materialism and commercialism of Christmas present.
>
> Steve Otfinoski, *The Golden Age of Novelty Songs*

An ethnic comedian specializing in exaggerated Swedish and other accents, Yogi Yorgesson reached the charts with two satirical holiday songs on Capitol Records in 1949: "Yingle Bells" (number five on the *Billboard* pop chart) and "I Yust Go Nuts at Christmas" (number seven). Both songs would be revived with *Stan and Doug Yust Go Nuts at Christmas* in 1970; "I Yust Go Nuts at Christmas" was eventually collected on *Dr. Demento Presents: Greatest Christmas Novelty* (1987). Both sides of Yorgesson's holiday single incorporated parodies of Christmas texts: "Jingle Bells" (1857) and "A Visit from St. Nicholas" (1823).

In Yorgesson's reimagining, "Jingle Bells" is altered from a joyful sleigh ride (one that probably had been taken by young boys and girls wishing to spend time together) to a winter trial to be endured by a couple of old fogies. Instead of a Currier and Ives backdrop filled with happy ice skaters and horse-drawn sleighs, the listener is left with an older married couple's poorly planned outing in the frozen backwoods. It helps that Yorgesson, whatever

FIGURE 6.3. Currier and Ives, "A 'Spill Out' on the Snow," ca. 1870. Print: lithograph. Library of Congress.

his age at the time that he cut the single, sounds like the old fogy he is singing about. The old-fashioned organ in the background tops the production, lending a cheesy air to the proceedings.

"Yingle Bells" begins innocently enough, with the wife asking her husband to leave the car ("coup-y") behind and to hitch up the horse: perhaps it will be just like an old-fashioned Christmas. The horse, however, is none too happy about the prospect of pulling the sleigh, and the couple's problems are just beginning: a sleigh ride through the countryside, the husband-narrator tells the listener, is just not what it used to be. As the couple dashes through the open air, the horse kicks up snow as the wind blows fiercely in the couple's face, leaving them chilled to the bone (the husband wishes he had remembered his long underwear). As it grows dark, the unpleasant ride becomes more unpleasant. The husband can no longer see where he is going (he thinks that his eyeballs may have frozen), and worse, he seems to have lost his wife during a turn at the Johnsons' place (or so he surmises when he can no longer hear her yell). For the older couple, the joyful outing leaves the husband on the verge of pneumonia and the wife hating sleigh bells.

Besides offering a fun turn on a classic holiday song, "Yingle Bells" suggests that while riding in a horse-drawn sleigh may have been fun once (back in the good old days), the times have changed. From the movies (*Holiday Inn* and *Christmas in Connecticut*) to Christmas cards (Grandma Moses), holiday imagery remained preoccupied with horse-drawn sleighs, even though—during the 1940s—fewer and fewer people owned a horse (or even lived in a place where you could own one), much less a sleigh. Yorgesson also reminds the listener of the obvious: as beautiful as a white Christmas may be when viewed from the living room

FIGURE 6.4. *A Christmas Story*, 1983. Peter Billingsley, Ian Petrella, Darren McGavin, and Melinda Dillon. By permission of MGM/UA Entertainment/Photofest.

picture window, it is unpleasantly cold for those accustomed to modern conveniences like radiators and furnaces.

"I Yust Go Nuts at Christmas" cuts a broader satirical sweep than "Yingle Bells," taking a sardonic look at holiday shopping, excitable children, and family togetherness. Because of the exhilaration, the expenditure, and an excess of eggnog, Christmas seems literally to drive the husband-father nuts. In the opening section, he lists a litany of familiar holiday problems. Because he has no idea what size nightgown his wife wears, he will buy her the carpet sweeper; and while Christmas presents may fill his children with magical wonder, he will go "in the red" to purchase them. For many, these observations would have hit the mark during the late 1940s, and with a few changes (including dropping the fake Swedish accent), they could still register sixty years later.

What remains most fascinating about "I Yust Go Nuts at

Christmas" is its spoken middle section. Parodying "A Visit from St. Nicholas," the husband waits until the house is quiet to sneak out for a beer at the corner saloon. Instead, he ends up drinking a number (a dozen, he guesses) of Tom and Jerrys, a Michigan-Wisconsin eggnog variation. He is awoken early the next morning (even though he got home very late) by kids jumping on the bed, his belly, and his face. As the family goes downstairs and lights the tree, the husband is suffering from a terrible hangover magnified by an accident involving stepping on a skate. Just when life seems to be returning to normal, relatives descend on the house and mayhem ensues: arguments and fights take place as a radio announcer speaks of peace on earth, goodwill toward men. As the melody and music returns at the end of this section, the husband attempts to convince the listener that despite everything—debt, a hangover, screaming kids, and obnoxious relatives—he really likes Christmas. A sentiment expressed earlier, however, seems to hold more truth: he is glad that Christmas comes only once a year.

Behind Yorgesson's preposterous vocal style assuring the listener that this is all in good fun, the family-centered Christmas with Santa Claus as the guest of honor has been turned upside down and shaken. "I Yust Go Nuts at Christmas" implies that it is the father-husband who provides Christmas for the family, not a magical figure named Santa Claus. Despite a reliance on "A Visit from St. Nicholas," Santa Claus is never mentioned in "I Yust Go Nuts"; it is "Papa" who will be in "hock" and who will presumably have to work to pay off the debt. This aspect is underlined by mirroring "A Visit from St. Nicholas." While the domestic tranquility is overseen by the father-patriarch in Moore's poem, Yorgesson's father wishes for nothing more than a strong drink; while Moore's children are snugly tucked in bed and dreaming of Christmas treats, Yorgesson's children are loud and obnoxious, more a nuisance than a blessing. Perhaps unusual for the time period (1820s), Moore's poem offers a portrait of a nuclear family (as opposed to an extended family), seemingly secluded from neighbors and relatives as Christmas approaches; perhaps less unusual for the time period (1940s), Yorgesson's Christmas day borders on chaos that threatens to spill over into the street. If "A Visit from St. Nicholas" served as an idealized portrait of a Christmas from a middle-class patriarch's point of view, then "I Yust Go Nuts at Christmas" offered a peek at the holiday from a working-class husband's point of view.

It is illustrative to juxtapose the view of the American family in "Yingle Bells" and "I Yust Go Nuts at Christmas" with another depiction of family life during the 1940s, *A Christmas Story* (1983). Because the movie is set during the 1940s in an industrial town in Indiana, it becomes difficult—for anyone watching the movie on a DVD years after its release—to identify *A Christmas Story* as a 1980s movie; the film often leaves the impression of having been made during the 1940s. Even as an old-fashioned movie about an earlier time and place, however, the narration offers one clue to its source: since the narrator is looking back in time, this film could never have been made during the 1940s. Likewise, curse words are occasionally used (or suggested) that would not have been allowed in a 1940s movie. This is a Christmas film, then, about looking back on one's childhood during the 1940s. Tracing the source of the material (Jean Sheppard's *In God We Trust, All Others Pay Cash*) we have a fictional account of childhood in the 1940s written by the author during the 1960s and filmed during the 1980s.

In the depiction of family life in *A Christmas Story,* a father, mother, and two boys serve as good examples of the American

Dream because of their very ordinariness. Dad (Darren McGavin) works for a living, Mom (Melinda Dillon) stays at home, Ralphie (Peter Billingsley) wants a Red Ryder BB gun for Christmas, and Randy (Ian Parker) just wants to tag along with his older brother. The house they live in may be quite small by today's standards (the brothers share a room and the kitchen-dining room combo is cramped), and little oddities—a furnace that never quite works and frequent flat tires on the Oldsmobile—provide a humorous look at the minor trials of the working middle class. But none of this matters. Within a quaint and seemingly innocent time called the 1940s, the American experience is realized through family life. Whatever transpires each day (at work, at school), the family gathers each evening around the table as a family. Filtered through a nostalgic gaze, making a living, having a roof over your head, receiving the right Christmas present, and sharing a home-cooked meal at the end of the day *are* the realization of American life.

When the nostalgic distance falls away in "I Yust Go Nuts at Christmas," however, the family unit seems more of a drain—on finances and privacy—than a repository of emotional well-being. Yes, Yorgesson is certainly having fun by exaggerating what can go wrong at Christmas, but he is also describing what does go wrong; he may be touching on familiar complaints, but these complaints are familiar for a reason. Relatives did arrive, stay too long, and get into arguments with one another; fathers did sneak out for a drink and come home under the influence. Many within families did (and do) go "nuts" at Christmas, and while the jauntiness of Yorgesson's melody made light of the fact, the sardonic undercurrent of the words lingered. If an American Christmas equaled family togetherness, there was always the possibility of too much of a good thing.

"Grandma Got Run Over by a Reindeer" (1979)

> Besides sending up Santa, "Grandma" is a merciless satire of American family holiday togetherness, as Grandma's untimely demise on Christmas Eve barely dampens the family's capacity for beer, card playing, and football games.
>
> Steve Otfinoski, *The Golden Age of Novelty Songs*

THE EVENTUAL success of "Grandma Got Run Over by a Reindeer" served as a reminder of how Christmas songs behave differently than the average popular song. It would have been easy to describe Elmo and Patsy's holiday song as "cornpone" humor, cut from the same mold as *Hee-Haw* and the parodies of Homer and Jethro (a country music duo that parodied many Christmas songs). As such, it would have been easy to imagine "Grandma Got Run Over by a Reindeer" as appealing to a limited audience (country music listeners), becoming popular for a short period of time (in November and December of one holiday season), and then occasionally being played as a curious oldie. Instead, "Grandma Got Run Over by a Reindeer" was recorded and then rerecorded (perhaps twice) as Patsy and Elmo jumped from independently financed to nationally distributed by a major label. By the end of 1985, a cornpone song about a trashy holiday tragedy had beat out Crosby's "White Christmas" for three consecutive years as a radio favorite.[13] Like "White Christmas," "Grandma" had become a holiday classic.

As a comic song, the lyrics to "Grandma Got Run Over by a Reindeer" might be described as "kitchen-sink style" songwriting: author Randy Brooks seems to have thrown every familiar Christmas cliché into the song. We have a grandmother ("Over the River and Through the Woods"), Santa Claus ("A Visit from

St. Nicholas"), a reindeer (*Rudolph the Red-Nosed Reindeer*), a family gathered for Christmas (*It's a Wonderful Life*), and a cornucopia of familiar holiday items (eggnog, fig pudding, and snow). Since "Grandma" aims at satire or perhaps travesty, though, the end result has none of the warm and fuzzy glow of Nat King Cole's version of "The Christmas Song." Instead, the bad taste and black humor of "Grandma" more closely resemble an inverted version of the classic holiday song.

"Grandma" begins with the song's chorus, reporting the accident: the grandmother of the song has been run over by a reindeer, causing her death on Christmas Eve. The grandmother, then, is the victim of a hit-and-run accident, believed—by the song's narrator (apparently a grandson) and grandfather—to have been perpetrated by none other than Santa Claus and his reindeer. The climax of the story (Grandma's death by Santa), it seems, has been revealed at the very beginning of the song.

The first verse moves backward like a murder mystery, reporting—as though explaining to the authorities—what had happened right before the incident. After an evening of drinking an excessive amount of eggnog (like the father in "I Yust Go Nuts at Christmas") and forgetting to take her medication, the grandmother staggers outside (perhaps to retrieve her medicine). On Christmas morning, the family finds Grandma, marked by hoof prints and "claw" marks. Perhaps the oddest detail goes unmentioned: no one (including Grandpa) had bothered to find out whether the tipsy grandmother had made it home safely the night before.

The second verse focuses on the family's grief, specifically Grandpa's. Even while the holiday will no longer be the same

FIGURE 6.5. *Christmas Vacation*, 1989. Juliette Lewis, Chevy Chase, Beverly D'Angelo, and Johnny Galecki. By permission of Warner Bros./Photofest.

without Grandma, Grandpa spends his time drinking beer, playing cards, and watching football, seeming barely to notice that his wife is gone. The biggest dilemma the family (which is dressed in mourning clothes) seems to face, however, is whether to open up Grandma's gifts or take them back to the store. In the final verse, the Christmas meal has been laid on the table, presumably on Christmas Day—leaving the impression that the family went to the trouble to cook a traditional meal the *day* they discovered that Grandma had died in a hit-and-run accident. There is a goose and fig pudding, but despite the meal, the absence of Grandma remains: the silver candles would have matched the silver in Grandma's wig.

The very end of the lyric returns to the circumstances of Grandma's death. After noting that he has warned his neighbors of Santa and the reindeer (though presumably they would be out of danger until the following Christmas), the grandson delivers the oddest two lines of the song: no one should issue a driver's license to Santa Claus, a man who lives (plays) with elves and drives a sleigh. However the listener chooses to interpret these lines—that Santa Claus is out-of-touch with reality or simply that Santa Claus is a pervert—the end result is scathing to all North Pole traditions. Through the lens of "Grandma," the Santa Claus of *Miracle on 34th Street* really does belong in a nut house.

It is intriguing that while "Grandma" mocks American holiday tradition, it never touches upon the religious aspect of Christmas. The easy explanation for this is that Christmas as religion—the virgin birth, the newborn savior, and the Holy Family—are simply off limits to satire. "You're mocking some people's faith and their religious beliefs," notes radio music director Frankie Blue, "and they may take that a little too seriously."[14] Another explanation, however, is that there is no real need to satirize religion in "Grandma": the real sacred cows within an American Christmas, after all, are family and home. The American family and a place called home, the same fixtures that Bing Crosby longed to return to in "White Christmas" and "I'll Be Home for Christmas," have been skewered and roasted in "Grandma."

Part of the skewering is accomplished through class: the family within "Grandma" seems destined for Jeff Foxworthy redneck jokes. Instead of gathering around the Christmas tree to sing carols, members of this family drink excessively, watch football and play cards, and wear silver and blue tinted wigs. Indeed, if the song's narrative were turned into a newspaper headline—"Grandmother

Run Over by Reindeer on Christmas Eve"—it would read like a parody of a tabloid headline. (On January 7, 2003, the *Weekly World News* published a story titled, "Grandma, 86, Run Over by a Reindeer!" about a woman in Peterborough, England, who had been out caroling when a reindeer attacked her. A grandson presumably told the paper, '[N]ow every time we hear that stupid song, we'll remember our grandma.'")[15] The final straw is the family's lack of decorum: they cannot decide whether to open Grandma's presents or take them back to the store. The American family that had struggled to establish Christmas as a home celebration had fallen on hard times. The notion of a horse-drawn sleigh crossing the river to grandmother's house no longer held its nostalgic glow.

Songwriter Randy Brooks has noted that his original inspiration for "Grandma" came from Merle Haggard's "Grandma's Homemade Christmas Card" (1973). When Brooks had first heard Haggard's maudlin song, he believed that it would end with the grandmother's death. It did not. For fun, then, Brooks decided to write another song, this time including the death of the grandmother. Unlike a sad country song, however, Brooks laid out the story's beginning and end during the song's opening chorus: Grandma meets her untimely demise when the song has barely started. "Grandma" falls very much within country music tradition (story songs, cornpone humor), echoing the self-reflective "You Never Even Called Me by My Name," the "perfect country song" that humorously and proudly details many of the genre's clichés. Like a country music parody, "Grandma" openly embraces its stupidity, inviting listeners to laugh at Grandma's lower-class origins while also laughing at themselves.

"Grandma," however, spread far beyond country music listeners, reaching other *Billboard* charts and, through video, television viewers (MTV). The video in particular matched the absurdity of the song, underpinning the negative portrayal of the family to an audience unfamiliar with country music parody. Besides offering insiders (country music fans) a chance to laugh at themselves by laughing at Grandma, the song also trashed (very publicly) the most sacred symbol of an American Christmas: the family.

The "Grandma" video begins with the camera pulling back from a roaring fireplace, revealing the family on Christmas Eve. The living room might be described as crowded fifties kitsch, with a cut-out "MERRY CHRISTMAS," a glitzy tree, and mismatched stockings on the congested mantel. The family portrait setting, which will return at the video's end, breaks up as members make an effort to prevent Grandma—staggering badly and carrying an empty flask—from going out into a snowstorm. Grandpa, meanwhile, is oblivious: covered with a newspaper, he seems satisfied to take a nap on the couch. Perhaps attempting to retrieve her medication, Grandma steps outside into the blinding snowstorm.

The following morning (after the attack), two police officers appear in the family's living room to take testimony, and one is holding Grandma's wig with the incriminating hoof prints. Grandpa seems dismayed and downhearted, or at least he does until he catches a peek at Cousin Mel's cleavage as she attempts to comfort him.

One might imagine that a video based on the recurrent non-idea of a grandmother being run over by a reindeer might lose steam after two minutes, but the "Grandma" video continues to have fun with itself through the very last frame. In one segment, a boy and a girl play with a miniature set (a house, figurines), re-enacting Grandma's tragedy. A snowman serves as a replacement for Grandma, standing before the family home, and the little girl sprinkles snow on the scene as the boy runs the symbolic grandmother down with a miniature sleigh driven by Santa and pulled by reindeer. Knocking Grandma over, they turn to one another and smile.

The biggest surprise, however, is saved until the end of the last verse (when the grandson warns all his neighbors of the danger): at this point, Grandma herself makes an appearance, back from the dead it might seem. Dropping down the chimney, she looks much as she did at the beginning of the video save for two changes: she is wearing a Santa Claus cap and, thanks to the chimney, is covered with soot and ashes. Even as she reappears, Grandpa ignores her to shower attention on Cousin Mel (who does not seem to mind). As the "Grandma" video comes to a close, the family and police officers gather beside the Christmas tree for another family portrait moment.

To heighten the absurdity of the "Grandma" video, professionalism has been tossed out the window. None of the lip syncs even attempt to match, the narrative (seemingly provided by the grandson) is tossed willy-nilly between family members, and Elmo himself (never attempting to look like more than a man cross-dressing as an older woman) plays Grandma. The entire enterprise leaves the impression of being acted and recorded by amateurs on a tight budget (which seems, historically, to be pretty much how the video was filmed).

It is instructive to place the view of the American family in "Grandma" beside another family portrait in *Christmas Vacation* (1989). The broad satire of *Christmas Vacation* captures the zeitgeist of the 1980s. While the film is set in a contemporary American suburb, Clark Griswold (Chevy Chase) seems determined to live out his life in a style befitting the 1950s. His attempt to do so involves the celebration of Christmas as a family holiday with all of the traditional trappings: an overdecorated house, an extended family crowded together under one roof, and a large meal prepared by the women of the family. Even his materialistic Christmas wish—to have a swimming pool built in the backyard—is designed to make his family happy and provide a reason for more togetherness. As a co-worker tells him, "You're the last true family man."[16]

Despite the broad satire of *Christmas Vacation*—the excessive decorations, the bickering families, and a series of disasters that nearly demolishes the Griswold home—the movie remains devoted to the rightness of traditional values centered on family and home. Clark's heart is in the right place, and despite everything that goes wrong, he succeeds in the end—as a father, husband, son, and new patriarch of the extended family—in pulling off an old-fashioned Christmas. Clark Griswold may work for a faceless corporation and live in an anonymous suburb; he may own a large house and, with his generous Christmas bonus, now be able to add a swimming pool; and he may embrace all the material trappings of modern consumer culture. But because of Clark's commitment to family and family life, his aspirations are deemed authentic, and this becomes very clear when he is compared to his two yuppie neighbors.

The yuppie neighbors are obsessed with high-end consumer products and driven to distraction by stains on the carpet; even a healthy habit like exercise reveals them as obsessively self-centered. Unnaturally, the couple has no children. For good measure, the male yuppie—Todd (Nicholas Guest)—refuses to defend his partner when she (Julia Louis-Dreyfus) is insulted, bringing his masculinity into question. Like *A Christmas Story, Christmas Vacation* has little interest in religion; unlike *A Christmas Story,* however, *Christmas Vacation* does draw a line: while consumption in itself is not wrong, there are good and bad forms of it.

Two other incidents within *Christmas Vacation* help underpin the American essence of the holiday. During the big family meal, Clark asks the family's eldest aunt (Mae Questel) to say grace. Confused (she seems to be suffering from some kind of dementia), she begins to say the Pledge of Allegiance. Later in the movie this moment is echoed. When an explosion on the family's lawn sends the plastic Santa Claus and reindeer flying, the aunt begins singing "The Star-Spangled Banner." In both instances, others join the recitation-singing as though acting on reflex. These funny moments juxtapose traditional religion (the prayer and the singing of carols) with patriotic pledges and songs, offering the latter as a replacement for tired, overworked sacred images. Within a contemporary American Christmas, the combination of family and consumption not only respects tradition but also qualifies as patriotic. Here, the vision of an American Christmas is little different from the ideal portrayed at the end of *Miracle on 34th Street* in 1947.

Unlike the middle-class Griswolds, the family depicted in the complete "Grandma" experience (song and video) might be kindly referred to as working class, as a euphemism for white trash, blue collar, or redneck (within the video, Grandma and Grandpa seem a little trashier than the rest of the family). Unlike the Griswolds, this was a family to laugh at, not with; if this was an example of the American family, one might surmise, God help us all. The absurdity of the family in the song is reinforced by the even greater absurdity of the family in the video, leaving onlookers with as unattractive a portrait of the American family as one might hope to find. With a family like this, it would be unlikely that Bing Crosby (or anybody else) would wish to come home for Christmas.

"Christmas at Ground Zero" (1986)

It would have been easy to imagine that "Grandma Got Run Over by a Reindeer" had taken the satirical holiday song as far as it could go. With "Christmas at Ground Zero," however, Weird Al Yankovic pushed the holiday song into the most unlikely of categories: apocalyptic horror. "Christmas at Ground Zero" appeared on Weird Al's *Polka Party* album in 1986, and a video for the song received airplay on MTV. It has been noted that the heavy satire of "Christmas at Ground Zero" was perhaps at odds with most of Weird Al's work: in general, his parodies and originals lightly poke fun at popular culture ("Like a Surgeon," "I Lost on Jeopardy"). In contrast, "Christmas at Ground Zero" offered a darkly tinted view of the American landscape during the 1980s, showing an America where everyone continued to smile and sing holiday carols—even as the nuclear warheads were falling.

One of the oddest aspects of "Christmas at Ground Zero," and an element that adds distance between it and most of the songs covered in this book, is the contrast between the music and the lyrics (the closest similarity occurs in "Christmas Time Is Here," with a children's choir singing happy lyrics languidly). While most Christmas songs attempt to match the mood of the words and melody, the music and lyrics of "Christmas at Ground Zero" are going in two different directions. The upbeat recording has been described as imitating the girl-group style from the early to mid-1960s and is reminiscent of material from holiday albums such as *A Christmas Gift for You from Phil Spector* (1963). The lyric, however, is pure black comedy, detailing a nuclear holocaust as Christmas bells chime. The strange mixture gives the impression of the Shirelles singing a lyric written by comedian Lenny Bruce. When we listen to the tone of "Christmas at Ground Zero" along with Weird Al's vocal, all seems cheery and bright; when we listen to the lyrics, it is the end of the world—as R.E.M. echoed the following year (1987)—as we know it.

The "ground zero" of Weird Al's title and opening line has a historical basis, though it will forever be confused with the collapse of the World Trade Center in 2001. (After journalists began referring to ground zero in relation to the World Trade Center, some radio stations apparently banned "Christmas at Ground Zero.") Originally, the phrase *ground zero* was adopted during World

FIGURE 6.6. *The Atomic Café*, 1982. Printed by permission of Libra Films/Photofest.

War II as the ground right below the place where an atom bomb detonated. Name checking ground zero, then, was to reference a nuclear explosion. Following the nuclear explosions in Japan in 1945, the phrase became commonly used.

The multiple bells (a seemingly larger bell and sleigh bells) that ring at the beginning of "Christmas at Ground Zero" leave the impression of a sound pastiche for the opening of a classic Christmas movie or song. Indeed, images of a larger bell followed by the ringing of sleigh bells open *It's a Wonderful Life,* while sleigh bells open Bing Crosby's version of "It's Beginning to Look a Lot Like Christmas." The happy sounds—including a clopping noise, perhaps simulating horses' hooves—are soon joined, however, by the whistle of a falling bomb. That it is, indeed, the whistle of a falling bomb is soon confirmed when an explosion rings out. This is followed by the joyous sounds of Weird Al's band, including a honking saxophone circa 1960. This entire setup unfolds within the first twenty-eight seconds of the song, before Weird Al has sung a syllable of the lyric.

Weird Al sings happily of Christmas cheer, panic, and disaster, as though Americans—until the bitter end—will do their best to carry on as usual. In the opening stanza images of sleigh bells and carolers mingle with blaring air-raid sirens; later, Weird Al will optimistically envision trimming the tree while dodging falling debris. Since the radio has confirmed the apocalyptic reality, there will be no time for last-minute Christmas shopping; and while many of the trappings of the holiday may remain (Jack Frost, reindeer footprints on the housetop), the listener is warned to load his or her gun in preparation for anything that comes down the chimney. Weird Al even manages to reference Christmas romance, with lovers ducking (as in the 1950s public service films that trained citizens to duck and cover from nuclear fallout) beneath mistletoe. Throughout the lyric, Weird Al happily meshes these jarring images together.

Looked at from the viewpoint of 1986, Weird Al's "Christmas at Ground Zero" could easily be interpreted as expressing more concern with the policies of the Reagan administration than with Christmas. As with many of Reagan's critics, Weird Al suggests that the current military policies of the administration have increased the likelihood of annihilation through nuclear war. This criticism becomes even more direct in the video for "Christmas at Ground Zero," which includes a clip of Reagan in front of a Christmas tree. Likewise, "Christmas at Ground Zero" suggests that the average consumer—in Reagan's "Morning in America"—could not care less. In the midst of the nuclear explosions and fallout, the song suggests, the only thing that bothers the average consumer is inconvenience: a nuclear war would interrupt Christmas shopping.

Considering the longer historical view, however, "Christmas at Ground Zero" serves as a broader condemnation of everything sacred about America's favorite holiday. Within Weird Al's three-minute satire, every holiday cliché—sleigh bells, carols, Jack Frost, shopping, Christmas trees, and Santa Claus—is joyfully dismantled and soon to be blown to smithereens. "Christmas at Ground Zero" also makes its point by evoking an earlier time and place (the 1950s) and undercutting the nostalgia of the ideal as imagined from a 1980s vantage point. In place of fondly recalled images from *Leave It to Beaver* and *Father Knows Best,* Weird Al reveals an apocalyptic horror only barely concealed by the symmetrical tree-lined streets of suburbia.

If "Grandma Got Run Over by a Reindeer" revealed the working class family gone-to-hell-in-a-handbasket, "Christmas at

Ground Zero" uncovered the 1950s that no one wished to remember; if "Grandma" came at the end of two decades of decline in the traditional family, "Christmas at Ground Zero" arrived six years into the decade that tried to revive the institution.

In the video for "Christmas at Ground Zero," Weird Al relies heavily on vintage footage, including parts of the famous (or infamous) Civil Defense film, *Duck and Cover* (1951). Part of the joke of the video, and one made apparent by the earlier documentary *Atomic Café* (1982), was how ineffectual duck and cover would have been at protecting anyone during a real nuclear explosion. As in the lyrics, the video for "Christmas at Ground Zero" contrasts images of atomic explosions with dated footage of an American Christmas; children duck and cover at school and anticipate the presents beneath the Christmas tree at home. The video, in fact, makes the connection to the past even more overt: much of the film footage is black and white while even the color footage leaves the impression of being several decades old (as in home movies and outdated film stock).

Sections of the video for "Christmas at Ground Zero" have an air of unreality. While the Americans within these segments are recognizable as such, many of their customs render them absurd, as though captured in an anthropological film. This is especially true when adults appear: American life and Americans seem quaint and unlikely to evoke nostalgia. As a woman knits and listens unemotionally to the radio, she appears oblivious to the holocaust that is occurring. While Christmas may retain many of its warm and fuzzy qualities, then American culture and Americans themselves are often rendered ridiculous. The viewer is invited to laugh at the culture, not with it.

Like Weird Al's "Christmas at Ground Zero," Joe Dante's

Gremlins (1984) combines humor and satire to take a wider swipe at America's favorite holiday. As the makers (Dante and others) note on the commentary track on the DVD version of *Gremlins,* the movie appears to imaginatively combine parts of *It's a Wonderful Life* (1947) with *The Birds* (1961).

Like *It's a Wonderful Life, Gremlins* is a portrait of small town life, with the economically depressed Kingston Falls filling in for the earlier Bedford Falls (there is a clip of *It's a Wonderful Life* playing on a small television set early in *Gremlins*). The plot revolves around the Christmas gift from father Randall Peltzer (Hoyt Axton) to son Billy (Zack Galligan); a Mogwai (known as Gizmo), a cute furry critter bought from a Chinatown shop. Gizmo's offspring (created from spilled water), however, are less warm and cuddly, and when fed after midnight become comically nightmarish. At once cleverly malevolent and unrestrained, the Gremlins unleash anarchy when they invade downtown Kingston Falls: they drink, smoke, eat candy, watch movies, dance, and fight (sex seems to be the one vice they show little interest in). They behave, then, like the average tweener hanging out at the local mall, or, more apropos to the setting of *Gremlins,* like the typical American consumer at Christmas.

Even though the heroes prevail, the gremlins—in short order—all but destroy downtown Kingston Falls. If Kingston Falls is an updated copy of Bedford Falls, then the devastated town is a copy of George Bailey's nightmare version of Bedford Falls (Pottersville) had he never existed. The difference, however, is that Kingston Falls really has been destroyed by stand-ins for rampaging consumers, stripped of ego and superego. Within *Gremlins,* small town America and all that it stands for has been finally laid to rest, the materialization of Bailey's nightmare.

If "I Yust Go Nuts at Christmas" and "Grandma Got Run Over by a Reindeer" revealed the underside of the American family, "Christmas at Ground Zero" revealed the underside of American society. Here, Americans are unmindful of the world around them, a mindlessness that reflects their political choices. Weird Al's slap-happy performance indicates the indifference of Americans to the real world; they only panic when the bombs start falling. Perversely, the upbeat vocal also adds a malicious undertow to the lyrics: Weird Al's performance or reading of the lyric leaves the impression that Americans are getting pretty much what they deserve. Like *Gremlins,* "Christmas at Ground Zero" is about the leveling of American Christmas culture, ostensibly brought down by a nuclear holocaust, though in reality brought down by self-absorption and unrestrained consumption.

FIGURE 6.7. *Gremlins,* 1984. By permission of Warner Bros./Photofest.

The Ghost of Christmas Future

> "Grandma Got Run Over by a Reindeer" was effectively the last Christmas novelty to create a major stir on the pop charts. With changing musical tastes, novelty records in general were an endangered species by the late 1970s.
>
> Steve Otfinkoski, *The Golden Age of Christmas Songs*

> I won't begrudge a single one of you for cringing when your drug store begins piping in holiday muzak sometime after Halloween, or longing for the day when our national nightmare of "Grandma Got Run Over By A Reindeer" will be over.
>
> Scott Frampton

IN 1985, a disc jockey at KLLR in Davenport, Iowa, with the unlikely name of Jack Daniels got fired for a holiday stunt: he had decided to play "Grandma Got Run Over by a Reindeer" over and over for the entirety of his four-hour shift. When management reached him by phone, he was told to quit playing the song. Daniels changed records but only for three songs before switching back to "Grandma." After playing "Grandma" approximately twenty-seven times between 5:30 a.m. and 8:50 a.m., Daniels was physically removed from the studio booth. Only the intervention of the songwriter Randy Brooks and performers Elmo and Patsy saved Daniels's job. The disc jockey had only been feeling low, after all, and had believed that "Grandma" would put him in the Christmas spirit.

It is worth noting that Brooks originally wrote "Grandma" around 1976–77 and that Elmo and Patsy first recorded it independently in 1979. By that time, the Christmas song (and Christmas in general) had lost much of its prestige and centrality within American culture. The Christmas song had survived many changes during the 1940s and 1950s, from the excesses of carnival to the onslaught of rock and roll. After 1963, however, the culture changed so radically as to signify a historic break. These changes were reflected within the music industry and would have a direct impact on the holiday song during the 1960s. Dave Marsh and Steve Propes write:

> After the British Invasion, the music itself changed almost immediately, with consequences so far-reaching that we're essentially still living in their aftermath. If all Christmas music can be divided into the period before Berlin gave Crosby "White Christmas" and the period after, all of popular music to this very day can basically be divided into the periods before and after the Beatles and their brethren reached the States.[17]

When the 1970s dawned, the music scene—in regard to Christmas—was no brighter. Marsh and Propes continue:

> The Christmas season became progressively less important; although it was still the most lucrative time of year to release a star's album, records now began to be marketed on more of a year-round basis. And with everybody—rockers, soft and hard, funkateers, discolettes—insisting on using their songs as vehicles for personal intimacies and expressive, often exhibitionist, individualism, the community of good cheer and warm family feeling that Christmas songs evoked came to seem more and more anachronistic.[18]

Within the mainstream during this era, holiday songs were old-fashioned, relegated to children and those old enough to remember the originals.

Following Kennedy's assassination at the end of 1963, the tumult of social and political events proved equally disruptive to the status quo. By the end of the 1970s, following Vietnam's inglorious end, Nixon's resignation, gasoline shortages, and stagflation, Americans may very well have suffered from the "malaise" of which President Carter spoke. This culminated on November 4, 1979, after fifty-two American embassy workers were taken hostage in Iran. Speaking at the Pageant of Peace, Carter told Americans:

> Christmas means a lot of things. It means love. It means warmth. It means friendship. It means family. It means joy. It means light. But everyone this Christmas will not be experiencing those deep feelings. At this moment there are 50 Americans who don't have freedom, who don't have joy, and who don't have warmth, who don't have their families with them. And there are 50 American families in this Nation who also will not experience all the joys and the light and the happiness of Christmas.[19]

These words found faith in the American way at its nadir, too worn down—by the economy, world events, and the weight of recent history—to rise to the occasion.

Carter's mention of family also name-checked another American institution that had fallen into disrepair by the end of the 1970s. Writing about the changes in the American family, Steven Mintz and Susan Kellogg note:

> A generation ago Ozzie, Harriet, David, and Ricky Nelson epitomized the American family. Over 70 percent of all American households in 1960 were like the Nelsons: made up of dad the breadwinner, mom the homemaker, and their children. Today, less than three decades later, "traditional" families

> consisting of a breadwinner father, a housewife mother, and one or more dependent children account for less than 15 percent of the nation's households.[20]

Divorce rates climbed steadily along with households headed by women and couples who chose not to marry. All of these phenomena equaled—across the cultural spectrum—a reshuffling of what constituted family. "What Americans have witnessed since 1960," Mintz and Kellogg write, "are fundamental challenges to the forms, ideals, and role expectations that have defined the family for the last century and a half."[21] Because women had often played *the* central role in arranging the family holiday celebration (shopping, cooking, decorating, and sending cards), these changes had a profound impact on an American Christmas.

If "Grandma" had receded in the rearview mirror like "Yingle Bells" or only appealed to a narrower group of listeners like "Christmas at Ground Zero," it would have been easier to ignore as a cultural barometer. Even in the early 1980s, however, before "Grandma" reached the charts, there were warning signs of the song's appeal. Rudy Uribe, the program director of KLAC-AM in Los Angeles, told *Billboard* in 1981, "We had more requests last year for a single by Elmo and Patsy called 'Grandma Got Run Over by a Reindeer' than we did for 'White Christmas.'"[22] In 1985, after the song had become popular, a *Billboard* headline announced, "Grandma Runs Over Bing in Holiday Race." Paul Grein opened his article by noting, "For the third consecutive year, Elmo & Patsy's novelty hit 'Grandma Got Run Over by a Reindeer' has nosed out Bing Crosby's classic 'White Christmas' as the season's most popular Christmas single."[23]

With "Grandma," the gentle ridicule of "Yingle Bells" and "I Yust Go Nuts at Christmas" had turned into scathing satire, razing (or accidentally knocking over) every sacred cow that the classic holiday song had celebrated between 1942 and 1963. Weird Al's vision of Christmas in America may have been darker in "Christmas at Ground Zero" (and would grow darker still in "The Night Santa Went Crazy"), but it followed in the aftermath of "Grandma." A traditional Christmas beside the fireplace with Crosby, Como, and Cole would have been a pleasant diversion during the 1960s and 1970s, but contemporary American life could no longer support the innocence and belief necessary for that kind of holiday.

If "White Christmas" had reminded the American soldier of the intangibles (family and home) he was fighting for, "Grandma" was described as "the tale of an inebriated granny who gets trampled by Santa and his sleigh when she staggers outdoors against the advice of family."[24] If "White Christmas" had embodied a deep and abiding faith in the American way of life, "Grandma" made light of the dreams and beliefs that Americans could no longer embrace wholeheartedly.

As such, "Grandma" became the anti-"White Christmas," the inversion of all holiday values and the end of the line for the national holiday song. "One way or another . . . ," write Marsh and Propes, "the success of Elmo and Patsy suggests the dire straits Christmas music had fallen into by the early 1980s."[25] No one, after all, listened to "Grandma" and reminisced about the old home place. Formed out of the dregs of seventies cynicism, "Grandma" announced—some twenty years late—the death of the popular American Christmas song.

FIGURE 7.1. "Crosby Family on *The Hollywood Palace* (ABC)," 1966. Son Harry Lillis Jr., Bing Crosby, son Nathaniel, wife Kathryn, and daughter Mary Frances. By permission of ABC/Photofest.

7

The New Nostalgia

The
paradox of the modern
American family is that while
we attach far greater psychological and
ideological significance to a happy family life than
did our ancestors, our work lives, our emphasis on
personal fulfillment, and our political behavior all
conflict with strong, stable family bonds.

Steven Mintz and Susan Kellogg,
Domestic Revolutions

[W]hatever may
have been wrong with the
idealistic side of the American
Dream, it was lost in the shadow
of the mindboggling abundance
of the material side of the dream.

Wilber W. Caldwell,
Cynicism and the Evolution
of the American Dream

To
buy a large
house also means more
work, time, and money to
maintain it; to buy an oversized
car means more effort and
money to drive it.

G. S. Evans

AFTER falling by the wayside during the tumult and confusion of the 1960s and 1970s, the Christmas song made a comeback during the more conservative 1980s. Even as "Grandma Got Run Over by a Reindeer" (1979) seemed the natural result of two decades of cynicism, Alabama's "Christmas in Dixie" (1982) resembled an updated, Southern version of "I'll Be Home for Christmas" (1943); and while *Gremlins* (1984) offered a nightmare inversion of *It's a Wonderful Life* (1946), *A Christmas Story* (1983) unabashedly embraced the 1940s as the good old days. By the time *A Very Special Christmas,* an album mostly featuring recordings of classic holiday songs by popular performers of the day (including the Pointer Sisters, Eurhythmics, Whitney Houston, Sting, and U2), was released in 1987, the message was clear: there was no need to update Christmas for the 1980s. All one needed to do was embrace Christmas past once again.

Like all popular culture, the Christmas song of the 1940s and 1950s reflected American values of the time or, more accurately, an idealized version of those values. The revival of these songs during the 1980s and beyond revealed that Americans continued to be attracted to these idealized values. The values were idealized in the sense that popular culture generally preferred espousing what listeners will agree with or find attractive as opposed to offering a serious critique of cultural practices. The American listener may have accepted a broad critique about celebrating the right kind of Christmas (an old-fashioned, a less-commercialized, and a kid-centered Christmas), but the sacred institutions that served as the foundations for an American Christmas—family, home, and a moderate level of consumption—had to be supported without reservations.

Looking back at the development of the Christmas song during the early 1940s, it is easy to wonder whether the holiday song was a happy accident or something American culture willed into existence. Obviously the success of "White Christmas" in 1942 and "I'll Be Home for Christmas" in 1943 inspired copycats for the remainder of the decade. These and other songs nonetheless played a specific role within American Christmas culture (as did the Christmas movie), explaining national mythology as it formed around the holiday. It was as though there was a specific need within the culture for Christmas songs.

On the surface, there was no reason that the everyday popular song could not have been spruced up for the winter season. All one needed were the typical trappings—shiny decorations draped over evergreens, brisk air and freshly fallen snow, and eggnog sipped beside a roaring fire—that distinctively marked the time of the year. And romantic themes worked well regardless of the season. Songs like "Baby, It's Cold Outside" and "Winter Wonderland," in fact, did just that, combining romance with seasonal trappings. Instead of designating a new category, these seasonal songs could have simply been labeled as "winter."

There was, however, an opportunity for holiday songs to address more substantial themes than romance set against a snowy landscape. As the modern era dawned in America (during World War II but especially afterwards), a booming economy and life in the suburbs would stretch, alter, and challenge earlier social and cultural patterns. Year round, these challenges were evident; but they became especially predominant during the eight-week winter holiday season. After World War II, Christmas operated like a cultural pressure cooker, requiring Americans to consume more in a compressed period of time. If consuming became the patriotic duty of every American, then Christmas became the new Fourth of July.

Within this pressure cooker, Americans attempted to maintain older beliefs and ideals: religious faith and a commitment to charity, the sanctity of home and family life, and the broader concepts of democracy and egalitarianism. And during the latter half of the 1940s and throughout the 1950s, they may have believed they had kept the faith. Increasingly, however, these older values had to be balanced against consumption and individualism, and as a result, a division formed between American ideals and everyday life. In his classic study of Christmas, James H. Barnett offers a similar binary. "It appears that the main ones [values] are brotherhood and family life. Both are traditional in Western civilization and are widely accepted in the Christian, Judaic, or humanistic traditions. However, they are in evident conflict with other powerful social values such as nationalism, individualism, and success."[1] The conflicts between these twin pillars, one spiritual and social minded, the other material and self-regarding, reached an apex during the Christmas season. Here, social pressure would push Americans to conform to a season filled with family, neighbors, and community on one side, and shopping, gift-giving, and self-gratification on the other.

While popular media (radio, records, magazines, comic books, and, by the late 1940s, television) may have reflected and offered a reasoned justification for the American way of life in general, traditional media—circa 1940—lacked a specific focus on Christmas. In essence, a gap developed between the growth of Christmas culture and the ability of popular media to support and reflect the new ideology. The modern Christmas song helped fill that gap.

The Genius of the Christmas Song

The genius of Christmas culture as conceived during the 1940s and 1950s was its openness toward the American experience. It is easy to point out in retrospect that the American celebration of Christmas had little to offer any group that fell outside of the mainstream; that Christmas was focused on family, home, and consumption as imagined by white, middle-class Americans; and that the ideal family was one that included a father and mother along with two or three children, while the ideal dwelling was a house magically transformed into a home within the suburbs. Many other aspects, heterosexual and patriarchal, would have been assumed. These concepts—we note when we take a historical look back—proved too narrow to define the American experience, even for the groups that supposedly bought into these values.

Undoubtedly many people were left out, if for no other reason than they lacked the economic means to participate in the American vision of a consumer-oriented Christmas. But this critique of Christmas circa 1950 fails to explain or comprehend the appeal of Christmas culture. While the American holiday had many shortcomings, the Christmas song nonetheless cast a very wide net within American society during the 1940s and 1950s.

Christmas songs reached millions of Americans across the boundaries of race, class, ethnicity, and gender between 1942 and 1963. It is often mentioned, as an example of the song's broad appeal, that Bing Crosby's "White Christmas" reached both the pop chart and the Harlem Hit Parade in 1942; this meant that "White Christmas" reached white and black listeners. African American groups like the Drifters also reached the charts with "White Christmas."

Christmas songs moved fluidly between genres, jumping from mainstream pop to R&B and country and back again to mainstream pop. On the surface, genre hopping meant that many holiday songs reached mainstream listeners (pop), rural audiences (country), and urban centers (R&B). Beneath the surface, these individual audiences expanded beyond predictable classifications. Increasingly after 1950, young white listeners embraced R&B; likewise, as many rural listeners migrated to cities during and after World War II, country music traveled with them. A great deal of holiday music may have initially represented white middle-class values, but these songs encompassed expansive values to which many nonwhite middle-class Americans aspired.

Even in presentation, most holiday songs proved fluid and malleable. "Here Comes Santa Claus" and "Winter Wonderland" worked equally well when sung by men and women, and neither ethnic background nor racial makeup nor nationality seemed to matter. Encoded with mythic though imprecise ideals (from home and family to democracy and equality) and presumptions (material abundance), the lyrics and music of these songs proved adaptable. The American Christmas song may have failed to please everyone, but it generally spoke to and for a wide American audience during the 1940s and 1950s.

The openness of the holiday song also extended to its lyrics. In songs like "Have Yourself a Merry Little Christmas" and "I'll Be Home for Christmas," the words were painted with broad brushstrokes, at once offering a specific set of values while simultaneously leaving the smaller details to the individual listener. These words were painted in warm colors, setting forth a vision of home and family while leaving particulars—suburb or city, ranch or split-level house, tree-lined street or sidewalks, two or three children—for each mom and dad to sort out. The Christmas song had the advantage of being both expansive and personal, a precut American Dream with customizing options.

The American Christmas song partly achieved this universal quality by relying on familiar seasonal associations. Songwriters borrowed heavily from traditional Yuletide imagery, filling lyrics with evergreens and tinsel, holly and mistletoe, snow and snowmen, sleigh rides and jingle bells, and fireplaces and chestnuts. They also borrowed heavily from poets and authors (Washington Irving, Clement C. Moore, and Charles Dickens), illustrators (Currier and Ives, Thomas Nast, Norman Rockwell, and Haddon Sundblom), early Christmas songs ("Jingle Bells," "Jolly Old Saint Nicholas," and "Up on the House Top"), and even modern folklore (*Rudolph the Red-Nosed Reindeer*). By stitching together a smorgasbord of holiday standbys, the Christmas song became a patchwork of lived American memories.

In emphasizing such a well-worn and seemingly genuine treasure trove of holiday heritage, it was easy to overlook what these songwriters had left out of the Christmas song. In emphasizing the familiar, they had also chosen to ignore anything divisive or exclusive. Most pointedly, they chose to disregard religious imagery and stories of the sacred. In the golden age of the popular American Christmas song, from 1942 ("White Christmas") to 1963 ("Pretty Paper"), a traditional sacred Christmas is either omitted or given little more than general recognition. There were neither Wise Men following a star nor shepherds watching over flocks nor a Holy Family in "The Christmas Song" and "Santa Claus Is Comin' to Town," as there was no evidence of Christian theology—the Virgin birth, angels on high, and the baby Jesus in a manger—in "Have Yourself a Merry Little Christmas" and "Blue Christmas."

In the same way, these songwriters chose to ignore the history—even as it had developed within the United States—of the carol. Several favorites, "Away in a Manger," "We Three Kings," and "O Little Town of Bethlehem," had been written in America during the latter half of the nineteenth century. Religion, supposedly *the* ideological opposite of materialism within an American Christmas, had been banished from the Christmas song.

While potentially offending some Christians who emphasized these elements, the lack of sacred imagery allowed these songs to reach a diverse audience without relation to belief: no one was excluded because of religion. Even among Americans who embraced religion during the 1950s, notes historian LeRoy Ashby, few were dogmatic: "Although 95 percent of Americans said that they were religious, only 53 percent could identify even one of the Gospels in the Bible. Here was a kind of secularized faith, concerned less with sectarian doctrine than with the religion of America itself. It provided a sense of belonging and reassurance."[2] The narrator in *A Christmas Story*, describing his father's faith, puts it more prosaically: "Some men are Baptists, others Catholics; my father was an Oldsmobile man."[3] In choosing to overlook religion, the popular Christmas song reflected and reinforced this secularized faith.

Stripping religion from the holiday song, however, was—in the end—only neutralizing. Many Tin Pan Alley songwriters intuitively understood that too much religion of the wrong kind alienated the popular music listener. The unstated problem, then, was less about religion and more about how the popular Christmas song would define the American holiday experience. To do so, the Christmas song would have to dig deep into the values and beliefs that defined the holiday season within the broader American culture.

A Place Called Home

> All interpretations of Christmas acknowledge the central image of the family in its celebrations.
>
> Daniel Miller

> The emphasis on harmony, hearth and home versus the bleakness of the outside world is ideologically powerful.
>
> Sheila Whiteley

IN ORDER to make the Christmas song an annual ritual, songwriters had to condense the season into a handful of ideas that Americans embraced as wholeheartedly as baseball and apple pie. These beliefs were so much a part of everyday American life and so ritualized that no one questioned them: *this is just the way things are, this is common sense*. This is exactly what Irving Berlin, Gene Autry, and others did beginning in 1942. Drawing from a common and deeply felt heritage—the longing for home and the centrality of family set against the backdrop of separation during World War II—these songwriters completed a clever sleight of hand. Home and family would be inserted to replace the missing religious content; furthermore, the family and home would be imbued with the same sacred qualities as the Nativity and stable. These elements, and to a lesser degree a belief in material well-being, would define what was sacred within an American Christmas, what Americans held more dear than the faith of Pilgrims, Puritans, and protestants of all stripes.

The pull of home and family was perhaps most clearly on display in nostalgic songs like "White Christmas," "I'll Be Home for Christmas," "Have Yourself a Merry Little Christmas," and "(There's No Place Like) Home for the Holidays." In his book on "White Christmas," Jody Rosen calls attention to the song's deep roots in American soil: "For although 'White Christmas' is ostensibly a Christmas tune, deeper connections link it to another song genre, one of the oldest and most durable in American music: home songs, ballads of yearning for lost rustic abodes."[4] Borrowing from "Home on the Range" and "Home, Sweet Home," Berlin consecrated this American "yearning" as fully realized within the holy season of Christmas. Rosen writes: "Berlin's elegiac 'White Christmas' lyric ties the song explicitly to the home song tradition. All the conventions of the genre are here: the dream of a rustic idyll that is temporarily and geographically remote, images of pastoral serenity, the association of happy times in distant days with childhood innocence and wonder."[5] Under the influence of Christmas, the family home—spruced up with sprigs of holly, wreaths, and a Douglas fir—became the holy center of holiday celebrations, the place where Americans renewed ties and passed on traditions.

These ties and traditions were easy to trace to the 1820s, when the American middle class first struggled to establish a domestic Christmas. Noting the eclipse of a Christmas centered on carnival and the street, Stephen Nissenbaum writes "a new kind of holiday celebration, domestic and child-centered, had been fashioned and was now being claimed as the 'real' Christmas."[6] The domesticity was also reflected in Clement C. Moore's "A Visit from St. Nicholas" (1823) with a father, mother, and children (snug in bed), and likewise in Charles Dickens's *A Christmas Carol* (1843), with the large (six children), happy Cratchit family. "In simplest terms," writes Penne L. Restad in *Christmas in America*, "Americans molded the idea of home into a spiritual and metaphorical sanctuary from the awesome changes that modern life had brought them."[7]

FIGURE 7.2. *It's a Wonderful Life,* 1946. Larry Simms, Karolyn Grimes, Jimmy Hawkins, James Stewart, Donna Reed, and Carol Coombs. By permission of RKO/Photofest.

Americans would consciously build on this tradition during the 1940s and 1950s, making a religion out of the nuclear family. In *Domestic Revolutions,* Mintz and Kellogg explain the growth of the postwar family as a reaction to the Depression and World War II: "American families had experienced unprecedented strain, and now they turned away from public concerns and sought in private life satisfactions available nowhere else."[8] As with earlier Americans, the family and home would serve as a refuge from the outside world. By the 1950s, Mintz and Kellogg note, the centrality of family life became the expected norm:

> According to the editors of *McCall's* the defining characteristic of the ideal family was "togetherness," a "new and warmer

> way of life" in which women and men sought to achieve fulfillment "not as women alone or men alone, isolated from one another, but as a family sharing a common experience." Family togetherness quickly became a national ideal, seized upon by advertisers, ministers, and newspaper editors.[9]

The new, consecrated American family would be self-contained, meeting all the needs—economic, emotional, and spiritual—of all members.

These tenets were national in scope and evoked by President Harry Truman during the tree lighting ceremony in 1951. That year, Truman returned to his hometown of Independence, Missouri. "Mr. Truman has it in mind to stay . . . [at] home, with his wife and their daughter and the friends and relations who keep dropping in, for a few days after Christmas," noted the *Meriden Record* of the President's homecoming.[10] Speaking from a desk in the home of his wife's family, Truman told the American people:

> Christmas is the great home festival. It is the day in all the year which turns our thoughts toward home.
>
> And so I am spending Christmas in my old home in Independence with my family and friends. As the Christmas tree is lighted on the White House grounds in Washington, I am glad to send this greeting to all of my countrymen.[11]

Seemingly, this was a sentiment to which all Americans could relate.

In 1978, President Carter also returned home. In a series of photographs taken during the visit, President Carter is shown at his mother's home in Georgia, sitting in a modest living room filled with family members. The *Boca Raton News* noted of the visit:

"President Carter is celebrating Christmas Day with presents and family and a pot luck dinner at his mother-in-law's home."[12] Like all Americans, presidents longed to return to family and home during the Christmas season.

The emergence of the popular Christmas song—"White Christmas" in 1942 and "I'll Be Home for Christmas" in 1943—mirrored the explosive growth of marriages that had begun during World War II. Likewise, "Here Comes Santa Claus" in 1947 and "Rudolph the Red-Nosed Reindeer" in 1949 paralleled the start of the baby boom in 1946. Even while songs like "I Yust Go Nuts at Christmas" (1949) seemed to question the sanctity of home and family life, no one wanted to be alone like the protagonist of "Blue Christmas" (1949). After the war, millions of families made a down payment on a home in the suburbs, fulfilling dreams that had been laid aside because of depression and war. At no time would these homes be more central to family life than during Christmas, leading Americans to agree overwhelmingly when Perry Como sang, "(There's No Place Like) Home for the Holidays."

Consuming Christmas

> The contemporary American Christmas is not directly related to Christianity: it has actually become the holiday of a rival religion, the religion of global consumer capitalism.
>
> Max A. Myers

> It is no exaggeration to predict that the American economy would lapse into recession if no one bought Christmas presents this year.
>
> James Tracy

IN A SENSE, families had taken Bing Crosby's dreams to heart during the 1940s and 1950s, attempting to carve out a place where

Christmas was unaffected by modernity. Within the loving embrace of family and home, modern Americans—like their nineteenth-century ancestors—could provide a safe haven against the outside world. During Christmas, this meant that parents could negotiate—with the continued help of Santa Claus—the postwar consumer splurge, neutralizing the influence of the market. "In memories of many Americans whose recollections of the decade are limited to faded magazine photographs, old movies, and television reruns," write Mintz and Kellogg, "the 1950s stand out as the golden age of the American family, a reference point against which recent changes in family life can be measured."[13]

The Christmas song of the 1940s and 1950s reflected and supported these myths. Likewise, the proliferation of Christmas songs

FIGURE 7.3. "President Reagan and Nancy Reagan Decorating the Residence Christmas Tree," 1983. Ronald Reagan Library.

matched the intensified focus on the family during the 1950s. "The key songs of modern Christmas music, notably 'White Christmas,' 'Rudolph the Red-Nosed Reindeer,' and 'Merry Christmas, Baby,' sprang up in the forties," note Dave Marsh and Steven Propes. "But the fifties undoubtedly produced the greatest number of enduring Christmas records."[14] If the family was the new American religion, and Christmas the family's most sacred celebration, then holiday songs functioned as hymns.

The new religion of family and home, however, had an Achilles heel: when sketching out a vision of an American Christmas, songwriters had left out any details that distracted from the beauty of the illusion. Philosophy professor Scott C. Lowe, naming the commonly repeated clichés of the Christmas season, writes:

> The new fallen snow blankets the moonlit hills as sleigh bells jingle in the distance. Inside, the lights shine, the tinsel sparkles, all the ornaments are hung with care and presents are piled high under the tree. It's Christmas and there's magic in the air. Cousins and aunts and uncles and grandparents gather together from far and near for feast and fellowship, and maybe a little football, too. There will be delicious food, sweet treats, and a few spirits (of the alcoholic variety) as well. And presents, yes, lots of presents. It's the stuff of fond memories. It's Christmas just like Norman Rockwell or Charles Dickens pictured it.[15]

The perfect Christmas, however, remained perfect by leaving out as much as it included. As cultural historian Karal Ann Marling notes of "White Christmas," "It says nothing about the crush of crowds in the stores, about old anxieties rekindled as families come together, the gifts that Santa didn't bring, the airports clogged with holiday delays—the stuff of Christmas phobias and stress."[16] The most significant detail that these songwriters downplayed or misrepresented or simply avoided was the growing consumer culture and its potential impact on the family.

Americans had long believed that a fault line rested beneath the snowy Christmas landscape, but they had misidentified that fault line as the conflict between Christianity and consumer culture. The perpetuation of this belief helped conceal a more essential conflict: the clash between the home and the marketplace, between the model of the American family and the desire for consumer goods. Americans had been correct in assuming that the secular world was challenging the sacred one within Christmas culture, but they had misnamed—because of habit, tradition, and the roots of religion—what they held most holy.

The struggle can be understood as one of tradition, with the home serving as a refuge from the marketplace. The home was a place of safety and family unity, a space defined by domestic tranquility. In her history of an American Christmas, Penne L. Restad notes:

> Middle-class antebellum Americans, even as they tried to shape the public world about them into a more perfect and orderly place, looked to home and family for respite from its trials and challenges. Through their idealization of the private virtues of domesticity, they hoped not only to escape physically from the strains and stresses of the profane world outside their door but to satisfy their need for a place of comfort, piety, security, and spiritual unity.[17]

At best, this attempt to separate family from the outside world had a short shelf-life, providing no more than a temporary patch for a problem that would only grow as consumer culture expanded. At worst, the attempt to separate family from the outside world simply ignored the growing influence of the market.

This ideal division between home and market became especially problematic during Christmas, when middle-class parents showered consumer goods on children. Santa Claus may have "decontaminated" the market for parents, but the initial problem of influence multiplied: the market, under the guiding hand of Santa Claus, had carte blanche to enter the American home. In the twentieth century, movies, records, and radio further encroached on the sacred space of the home and family life. With modern media, advertising was broadcast directly into the home, bypassing traditional barriers of community, church, and family. With these permeable influences, no one knew where the lines between home and market began and ended.

The balance between home and the market was further complicated by the resources needed to maintain a modern Christmas. While family and home may have defined the sacred elements of Christmas for many Americans, the time and money required to generate and pay for the holiday equaled less time at home and less time with family. "No other celebration came close," writes Christmas historian William B. Waits, "to demanding the level of effort, money, and attention that Christmas did."[18]

Each family had to shop for and wrap gifts, decorate a tree and home, send cards and bake cookies, attend special functions, and prepare special meals. Even as a family prepared for the holiday, everyday responsibilities—children, laundry, grocery and household shopping, house and yard work, and miscellaneous errands—continued. From a financial and time standpoint, Christmas had to be celebrated within the constraints of everyday life.

"Working longer hours with record numbers of bankruptcies," writes James Tracy, "spending more time shopping and commuting and less time with their own children than ever before while their junk overflows into storage facilities, Americans, of course, pay a heavy price for this secular faith in legitimating oneself by dying with the most toys."[19]

Consumption could also undercut family unity in less obvious ways. Even though a family resided under the same roof, everyone consumed as individuals. As young baby boomers became a distinct market with control over their own money during the 1950s (whether earned or provided by parents), advertisers were more interested in demographics than family togetherness. Steven Mintz and Susan Kellogg note of baby boomers: "Increased affluence increased opportunities for education, travel, and leisure, all of which helped to heighten expectations of self-fulfillment. Unlike their parents, they had considerable expectations for their own material and emotional well-being."[20]

In the 1960s, this effect became even more pronounced. James Tracy writes:

> [T]he counterculture of the 1960s, far from being revolutionary, was, in fact, a consummate expression of the dominant culture—that immediate gratification without responsibility, sexual indulgence, primacy of leisure over work, and the commodification of experience (a drug available for every emotion) were more expressive of consumer capitalism than a revolt against it.[21]

While Americans clung to the idea of Christmas as family, individual habits of consumption helped splinter its reality.

The holiday songs that focused most clearly on consumption

were children's songs about Santa Claus, though even here, the focus was mostly implied. Children made lists, asked, and prayed for toys, and since they were only children, these wishes seemed more innocent than greedy. Even if a listener had considered that an adult—not Santa—had to pay for these gifts, these songs *were* children's songs. The songs themselves mimicked the wonder of a child anticipating Santa and presents, and as such expressed little concern with the realism of economics. Although these songs celebrated mountains of gifts piled around the tree, the economic element remained nonthreatening.

The influx of consumer culture and the strain it placed on the American family were deepened by a simple fact: Americans wanted to believe they could have it both ways. They wanted to believe they could step into—and back out of—consumer culture as it suited them; that there were good and bad forms of consumerism; that they could retain influence over children while filling the home with consumer goods; and that a group of people under the same roof could consume as individuals and still come together—especially at Christmas—as a family. Far from questioning these assumptions, the modern American holiday song supported these myths with few reservations. The delusion was so complete that even the Christmas song seemed unaware of itself as a commercial product.

The New Nostalgia

> Whether utopian or dystopian, the centrality of music in the Christmas ritual is arguably attributable to its potential to define (and later recapture) a mood.
>
> Sheila Whiteley

> Perhaps the first and most obvious thing to note about contemporary nostalgia is that it is very big business.
>
> Fred Davis, *Yearning for Yesterday*

THE nuclear family would face even greater challenges from consumer culture when Americans reembraced the Christmas song during the 1980s. In trying to put old wine in new bottles, however, Americans were in danger of reducing all Christmas music—regardless of song type—to nostalgia. Looking at how Americans viewed family life from the 1950s, Kathleen M. Sands writes:

> The fantasy was offered up to all America: this was how we used to be, how decent and wholesome, how cheerful and patriotic. Since the 1980s, with its new nostalgia for the presumed era of "traditional" American families, the fantasy has been doubled. Now the 1950s, which were themselves all about forgetting, have been memorialized as supposed touchstones for the prelapsarian American past.[22]

But as family historians Mintz and Kellogg, writing in 1987, note, this kind of nostalgia equaled little more than a dead end.

> There is little point in looking nostalgically to the past for a solution to current problems. The 1950s pattern of family life—characterized by high rates of marriage, high fertility, and stable rates of divorce—which many continue to regard as an ideal, was the product of a convergence of an unusual series of historical, demographic, and economic circumstances unlikely to return again.[23]

Undoubtedly, Christmas songs made people feel good by reflecting this ideal, but the original problem of outside influence had never been resolved; consumer culture still had the power to undermine the family and the home.

Indeed, one reason that Christmas and the Christmas song had lost its clout as a cultural unifier during the 1960s and 1970s was its attachment to the family. During the 1940s and 1950s, the idea of family was intimately and intricately connected with Christmas, to the point where the ritual of a family holiday seemed "natural." But as the fortunes of the American family declined, so did the centrality of Christmas. Mintz and Kellogg write:

> Since 1960 U.S. families have undergone a historical transformation as dramatic and far reaching as the one that took place at the beginning of the nineteenth century. Even a casual familiarity with census statistics suggests the profundity of the changes that have taken place in family life. Birthrates plummeted. The average number of children per family fell from 3.8 at the peak of the baby boom to less than 2 today [1987]. At the same time, the divorce rate soared. Today the number of divorces each year is twice as high as it was in 1966 and three times higher than in 1950. The rapid upsurge in the divorce rate contributed to a dramatic increase in the number of single-parent households, or what used to be known as "broken homes."[24]

While many Americans remained attached to the family after 1963, these social changes undercut the ideology on which modern Christmas culture—and the Christmas song—had been built. While holiday culture remained part of the mainstream, it was aimed at a narrower audience.

It is intriguing that much of the popular Christmas culture of the 1960s emerged as animated television specials targeted at

FIGURE 7.4. *Gremlins*, 1984. Zach Galligan, Frances Lee McCain, and Hoyt Axton. By permission of Warner Bros./Photofest.

children. While the family and extended family persisted in some of these specials, essential components seemed to be missing. In *Rudolph the Red-Nosed Reindeer* (1964), most of the male father figures—including Santa Claus—are overbearing. And while the conflicts within the story are resolved, much of the plot—Rudolph running away from home and the unwanted dolls on the Island of Misfit Toys—seems like a model for the dysfunctional family. The following year, *A Charlie Brown Christmas* disposed of parental figures altogether, leaving a group of neighborhood kids to cobble together a holiday out of a scrubby pine, a poorly executed Christmas play, and a few verses from Luke.

While other animated shows remained committed to the family, something fundamental had shifted. In the Max Fleischer version of *Rudolph the Red-Nosed Reindeer* from the 1940s, the young Rudolph stops to write a letter to his parents, letting them know that he will be busy helping Santa Claus. In 1970 in *Frosty the Snowman,* Frosty asks Karen (the young heroine of the story) if it will be okay for her to travel to the North Pole. She responds: "I'm sure my mother won't mind, as long as I'm home in time for supper." By the 1980s, the changes within the American family would be even more pronounced.

As *A Christmas Story* was attempting to evoke an old-fashioned holiday in 1983, a dark movie called *Gremlins* (1984) attempted to turn *It's a Wonderful Life* (1946) inside out. The American family is shown facing hard times in *Gremlins,* and it is far from clear whether love and family ties will be enough to save it. The head of the Peltzer family, Randall Peltzer (Hoyt Axton), is beloved by his son, Billy (Zach Galligan), and his wife, Lynn (Frances Lee McCain), though he is an incompetent inventor (nothing he invents works properly). He is a later day Edison, albeit a failed one with no place in contemporary America.

The final word on the fate of the American family, however, has been left to Kate Beringer (Phoebe Cates), Billy's love interest. Late in *Gremlins,* she delivers a monologue explaining why she hates the most American of all holidays, Christmas:

> The worst thing that ever happened to me was on Christmas. Oh, God. It was so horrible. It was Christmas Eve. I was nine years old. Me and Mom were decorating the tree, waiting for Dad to come home from work. A couple hours went by. Dad wasn't home. So Mom called the office. No answer. Christmas Day came and went, and still nothing. So the police began a search. Four or five days went by. Neither one of us could eat or sleep. Everything was falling apart. It was snowing outside. The house was freezing, so I went to try to light up the fire.

> That's when I noticed the smell. The firemen came and broke through the chimney top. And me and Mom were expecting them to pull out a dead cat or a bird. And instead they pulled out my father. He was dressed in a Santa Claus suit. He'd been climbing down the chimney on Christmas Eve, his arms loaded with presents. He was gonna surprise us. He slipped and broke his neck. He died instantly. And that's how I found out there was no Santa Claus.

Whether the traditional family had been defeated by the changes of the 1960s and 1970s or simply outlived its usefulness as a model, the father-breadwinner had been defeated by the demands of consumer culture. The idea that there was a man who dressed in a red suit and mysteriously delivered presents without monetary concern no longer seemed plausible.

During the golden age of the Christmas song (1942–1963) the lyrics, music, and performers of these songs offered an entrancing and expansive vision of American life. If the holiday song was overly optimistic—about the American way of life and about the future of America—it mirrored the zeitgeist of the era. Ultimately, however, the Christmas song failed the era and any future era that embraced it because it neglected one side of the modern American epic. By elevating the family and home and downplaying the role of consumption, it made American values appear to be in harmony. If this seemed naïve during the 1940s and 1950s, it had become delusional by the 1980s and beyond. Americans believed they could have it all: happy families and limitless consumer goods. Few—including the men and women who penned the classic Christmas songs—were willing to contradict them.

Acknowledgments

First I would like to thank my wife, Elizabeth C. S. Lankford, my first reader, who had to tolerate year-round Christmas music for the duration of this project. I am also grateful for the involvement and insight of my acquiring editor, Sian Hunter. Likewise, I would like to thank both Paul Mullins and Bruce David Forbes for reading and commenting on earlier versions of the manuscript.

A number of people at college and public libraries also aided my research: Stephanie Hunter and Winston Barham at the University of Virginia Music Library; Belinda Carroll at the Knight-Capron Library at Lynchburg College; Elisa Rollins, Candy Thompson, Candice Michalik, and Ken Morrison at the Lynchburg Public Library; and Jim Whalen at the J. Robert Jamerson Memorial Library in Appomattox, Virginia.

I would also like to thank my agent, Robert Lecker, for his help with developing and finally placing this project. And finally, I would like to thank Meredith Morris-Babb, Shannon McCarthy, Teal Amthor-Shaffer, Gillian Hillis, Ale Gasso, Michele Fiyak-Burkley, Claire Eder, and everyone at the University Press of Florida for their efforts on behalf of the book.

Notes

Chapter 1. The American Christmas Song

1. ASCAP, "ASCAP Announces Top 25 Holiday Songs," November 27, 2006, http://www.ascap.com/press/2006/112706_xmassongs.html.
2. "Have a 'Coke' = Merry Christmas," *Life*, December 18, 1944, 35.
3. Marsh and Propes, *Merry Christmas, Baby*, 8.
4. Hollis, *Christmas Wishes*, 81–84.
5. Whitburn, *Christmas in the Charts: 1920–2004*, 74.
6. Studwell, *Christmas Carol Reader*, 178–79.
7. Marsh and Propes, *Merry Christmas, Baby*, 9.
8. Hollis, *Christmas Wishes*, 85.
9. Marsh and Propes, *Merry Christmas, Baby*, 6.
10. Ibid., 7.
11. "Kringle Jingles Ring the Bell," *Billboard*, December 18, 1943.
12. Ibid.
13. Ashby, *With Amusement for All*, 270.
14. Marsh and Propes, *Merry Christmas, Baby*, 7.
15. Ibid., 3.
16. Forbes, *Christmas*, 142.
17. Barnett, *American Christmas*, 122.
18. Forbes, *Christmas*, 130.
19. Waits, *Modern Christmas in America*, 3.
20. Marling, *Merry Christmas!* 43.

Chapter 2. Nostalgia: Home for Christmas

1. Marsh and Propes, *Merry Christmas, Baby*, 10.
2. Ibid., 6.
3. Mark Glancy, "Dreaming of Christmas: Hollywood and the Second World War," in Connelly, ed., *Christmas at the Movies*, 64.
4. Marsh and Propes, *Merry Christmas, Baby*, 6.
5. Tarkington, *The Magnificent Ambersons*, 11–12.
6. Bridgman, *Within My Horizon*, 238.
7. Fred Davis, *Yearning for Yesterday*, 15.

8. Ibid., 102.
9. Ibid., 103.
10. Barnett, *American Christmas,* 59.
11. "Soldiers Say Farewell to Girls as Christmas Leaves Are Canceled," *Life,* December 15, 1941, 40.
12. Rosen, *White Christmas,* 141–42.
13. *I'll Be Home for Christmas,* 1–2.
14. Coontz, *The Way We Never Were,* 156–60.
15. Tindall, *America,* 1143.
16. Ennis, *Seventh Stream,* 121.
17. Morris, *Postscript to Yesterday,* xv.
18. Ibid., xxi.
19. Jezer, *Dark Ages,* 110.
20. Morris, *Postscript to Yesterday,* 446–47.
21. Rosen, *White Christmas,* 161.
22. Waggoner, *It's a Wonderful Christmas,* 46.
23. *Life,* December 15, 1941, 17.
24. "Kringle Jingles Ring the Bell," *Billboard,* December 18, 1943, 14.
25. Moses, *Grandma Moses,* 39.
26. Hugh Martin/Ralph Blane, "Have Yourself a Merry Little Christmas," http://www.hughmartin.com/have-yourself-a-merry-little-christmas.
27. David Vandermast, "Blighted Hopes," *American Scientist,* July–August 2008, http://www.americanscientist.org/bookshelf/pub/blighted-hopes.
28. Freinkel, *American Chestnut,* 18–24.
29. Rosen, *White Christmas,* 147.
30. Ashby, *With Amusement for All,* 267.
31. Ibid., 266.
32. Marling, *Merry Christmas!,* 328.
33. Seeley, *Season's Greetings from the White House,* 204.
34. Rosen, *White Christmas,* 147.
35. Marsh and Propes, *Merry Christmas, Baby,* 10.
36. Rosen, *White Christmas,* 146.

Chapter 3. Santa Claus: A Bag Full of Toys

1. Cohen, *Consumers' Republic,* 113.
2. Jezer, *Dark Ages,* 118.
3. McGovern, *Sold American,* 360.
4. Waits, *Modern Christmas in America,* 191.
5. Cohen, *Consumers' Republic,* 119.

6. Barnett, *American Christmas,* 88.
7. Waits, *Modern Christmas in America,* 195.
8. Cohen, *Consumers' Republic,* 114.
9. Forbes, *Christmas,* 90.
10. Waits, *Modern Christmas in America,* 120–33.
11. Cross, *The Cute and the Cool,* 90.
12. *Coca-Cola Collectible Santas,* 13.
13. Pendergrast, *For God, Country, and Coca-Cola,* 181.
14. Charles and Staples, *Dream of Santa,* 16.
15. Pendergrast, *For God, Country, and Coca-Cola,* 181.
16. Clement Clarke Moore, "A Visit from Saint Nicholas," 1823, in Gardner, ed., *The Annotated Night Before Christmas,* 39–42.
17. Charles and Staples, *Dream of Santa,* 82.
18. Ibid., 56–57.
19. *Coca-Cola Collectible Santas,* 11.
20. Hollis, *Christmas Wishes,* 85.
21. Belk, "A Child's Christmas in America," 94.
22. Ibid.
23. Zinsser, *Easy to Remember,* 37.
24. John Frederick Coots and Haven Gillespie, "Santa Claus Is Comin' to Town."
25. Belk, "A Child's Christmas in America," 90.
26. Cross, *The Cute and the Cool,* 91.
27. Dundes, *Christmas as a Reflection of American Culture,* 12.
28. Ibid., 19.
29. Dorson, "Yuletide Gift-Givers," 63.
30. Marsh and Propes, *Merry Christmas, Baby,* 16.
31. Barnett, *American Christmas;* Dundes, *Christmas as a Reflection of American Culture.*
32. Dundes, *Christmas as a Reflection of American Culture,* 20.
33. Mark Connelly, "Santa Claus: The Movie," in Connelly, ed., *Christmas at the Movies,* 124.
34. *Miracle on 34th Street,* directed by George Seaton, 1947.

Chapter 4. Carnival: Beneath the Mistletoe

1. Marsh and Propes, *Merry Christmas, Baby,* 9.
2. Nissenbaum, *Battle for Christmas,* 7–8.
3. Ibid., 6.
4. Burke, *Popular Culture in Early Modern Europe,* 264–65.

5. Nissenbaum, *Battle for Christmas,* 6.
6. Pleck, *Celebrating the Family,* 45.
7. Restad, *Christmas in America,* 9.
8. Pleck, *Celebrating the Family,* 45.
9. Nissenbaum, *Battle for Christmas,* 22.
10. Martell, ed., *American Christmases,* 12.
11. Schmidt, *Consumer Rites,* 23.
12. Nissenbaum, *Battle for Christmas,* 311.
13. Burke, *Popular Culture in Early Modern Europe,* 265.
14. Nissenbaum, *Battle for Christmas,* 313.
15. Ibid., 312.
16. Hall, "The Venereal Confronts the Venerable," 65.
17. *Christmas in Connecticut,* directed by Peter Godfrey, 1945.
18. Sheet music of Felix Bernard and Richard B. Smith, "Winter Wonderland."
19. Menendez and Menendez, *Christmas Songs Made in America,* 33.
20. Fred Danzig, "Dean Martin Show Typically Charming," *Beaver Valley Times,* January 13, 1960, 15.
21. William Ewald, "Martin Show Had a Lot of Charm," *Beaver Valley Times,* March 20, 1959, 16.
22. Thomas B. Congdon Jr., "Letter to the Editor," *Life,* December 29, 1952, 8.
23. Qutb, "America I Have Seen," 20.
24. Waggoner, *It's a Wonderful Christmas,* 91.
25. *Yes, Virginia, There Is a Santa Claus,* 130.
26. "Rock 'N Roll: A Frenzied Teen-Age Music Craze Kicks Up a Big Fuss," *Life,* April 18, 1955, 166.
27. Ibid., 166.
28. Ibid., 168.
29. "To Play Or Not to Play Is'?'" *Billboard,* December 16, 1957, 26.
30. Ibid., 26.
31. "Presley Record Played, So Disc Jockey Fired," *Tri City Herald,* December 5, 1957, 2.
32. "Elvis Fans Go Wild in Chicago," *St. Joseph's News-Press,* March 29, 1957, 2.
33. "Two 'Dolls' Want Elvis for Yule," *Portsmouth Times,* December 13, 1956, 12.
34. "Elvis Morally Insane, Minister Says," *Herald-Journal,* December 5, 1956, 16.

Chapter 5. The Blues and Hard Times: An American Carol

1. Diamond, "Singing Those Christmas Holiday Blues," 32.
2. Elizabeth Pleck, "Christmas in the Sixties," in Horsley and Tracy, eds., *Christmas Unwrapped,* 28–29.

3. Bowler, *World Encyclopedia of Christmas*, 25.
4. Dickens, *A Christmas Carol*, 5.
5. Ibid., 8.
6. Ibid., 3.
7. Ibid., 14.
8. Ibid., 65–66.
9. Ibid., 66.
10. Ibid., 68.
11. Ibid., 66.
12. Schmidt, *Consumer Rites*, 184.
13. Dickens, *A Christmas Carol*, 8.
14. Ibid., 8.
15. Ibid., 4.
16. Ibid., 40.
17. Ibid., 20.
18. Ibid., 21.
19. Ibid., 22.
20. Hearn, *The Annotated Christmas Carol*, 56.
21. Ibid., 62.
22. Dickens, *A Christmas Carol*, 27.
23. Ibid., 27.
24. Ibid., 28.
25. Basinger, *It's a Wonderful Life Book*, 196.
26. Ibid., 267.
27. Zinsser, *Easy to Remember*, 146.
28. "Folk," *Billboard*, December 4, 1948, 98.
29. Ibid., 28.
30. "Roy Orbison, Pretty Paper," *Billboard*, November 23, 1963, 14.
31. *I'll Be Seeing You*, directed by William Dieterle, 1945.
32. Chris Hutchins, "Hawker-Ifield Pen Follow-Up," *Billboard*, November 9, 1963, 26.
33. "Address to Congress Following Kennedy's Assassination," *PBS*, November 27, 1963, http://www.pbs.org/ladybird/epicenter/epicenter_doc_speech.html.
34. Elizabeth Pleck, "Christmas in the Sixties," in Horsley and Tracy, eds., *Christmas Unwrapped*, 19.
35. Diamond, "Singing Those Christmas Holiday Blues," 35.
36. Rosenthal, *Winter Blues*, 79–80.
37. Mendelson, with Melendez, *A Charlie Brown Christmas*, 113.
38. Dickens, *A Christmas Carol*, 56.

39. John Storey, "The Invention of the English Christmas," in Whiteley, ed., *Christmas, Ideology and Popular Culture,* 26.

Chapter 6. Satire: Surviving Christmas

1. Later, "settle our brains" often became "just settled down."
2. Clement Clarke Moore, "A Visit from St. Nicholas," in Gardner, ed., *The Annotated Night Before Christmas,* 39–40.
3. Gardner, ed., *The Annotated Night Before Christmas,* 46–47.
4. Ibid., 47.
5. Ibid., 48.
6. Ibid., 48.
7. Ibid., 48.
8. Ibid., 14.
9. Otfinoski, *Golden Age of Novelty Songs,* 197.
10. Ibid., 198.
11. Highet, *Anatomy of Satire,* 235.
12. Mark Connelly, "Santa Claus: The Movie," in Connelly, ed., *Christmas at the Movies,* 122.
13. Paul Grein, "'Grandma' Runs Over Bing in Holiday Race," *Billboard,* December 21, 1985, 57.
14. Denise Gorga, "Novelty Tune Brightens Season," *Ludington Daily News,* December 22, 1986, 9.
15. "Grandma, 86, Run Over by a Reindeer!" *Weekly World News,* January 7, 2003, 22.
16. *Christmas Vacation,* directed by Jeremiah S. Chechik, 1989.
17. Marsh and Propes, *Merry Christmas, Baby,* 64.
18. Ibid., 71.
19. Seeley, *Season's Greetings from the White House,* 213.
20. Mintz and Kellogg, *Domestic Revolutions,* 203.
21. Ibid., 204.
22. Robyn Wells, "Yule Songs Creep Into Programing," *Billboard,* November 21, 1981, 8.
23. Paul Grein, "'Grandma' Runs Over Bing in Holiday Race," *Billboard,* December 21, 1985, 57.
24. "Run-In with Reindeer Jingles Coins for Singers," *Sarasota Herald-Tribune,* December 13, 1979.
25. Marsh and Propes, *Merry Christmas, Baby,* 80.

Chapter 7. The New Nostalgia

1. Barnett, *American Christmas*, 139.
2. Ashby, *With Amusement for All*, 289.
3. *A Christmas Story*, directed by Bob Clark, 1983.
4. Rosen, *White Christmas*, 112.
5. Ibid., 113.
6. Nissenbaum, *Battle for Christmas*, 99.
7. Restad, *Christmas in America*, 42.
8. Mintz and Kellogg, *Domestic Revolutions*, 178.
9. Ibid., 180.
10. "President Due to Light National Christmas Tree," *Meriden Record*, December 24, 1951, 28.
11. Seeley, *Season's Greetings from the White House*, 206.
12. "Carters Enjoy Christmas at Home," *Boca Raton News*, December 25, 1978.
13. Mintz and Kellogg, *Domestic Revolutions*, 178.
14. Marsh and Propes, *Merry Christmas, Baby*, 21.
15. Lowe, ed., introduction to *Christmas*, 1.
16. Marling, *Merry Christmas!*, 328.
17. Restad, *Christmas in America*, 42.
18. Waits, *Modern Christmas in America*, 2.
19. James Tracy, "The Armistice over Christmas," in Horsley and Tracy, eds., *Christmas Unwrapped*, 15.
20. Mintz and Kellogg, *Domestic Revolutions*, 206.
21. James Tracy, "The Armistice over Christmas," in Horsley and Tracy, eds., *Christmas Unwrapped*, 15.
22. Kathleen M. Sands, "Still Dreaming: War, Memory, and Nostalgia in the American Christmas," in Horsley and Tracy, eds., *Christmas Unwrapped*, 55.
23. Mintz and Kellogg, *Domestic Revolutions*, 237.
24. Ibid., 203–4.

Bibliography

Ashby, LeRoy. *With Amusement for All: A History of American Popular Culture Since 1830*. Lexington: University Press of Kentucky, 2006.

Barnett, James H. *The American Christmas: A Study in National Culture*. New York: MacMillan, 1954. Reprint, New York: Arno, 1976.

Basinger, Jeanine. *The "It's a Wonderful Life" Book*. New York: Alfred A. Knopf, 1996.

Belk, Russell W. "A Child's Christmas in America: Santa Claus as Deity, Consumption as Religion." *Journal of American Culture* 10, no. 1 (Spring 1987): 87–100.

Bowler, Gerry. *The World Encyclopedia of Christmas*. Toronto: McClelland and Stewart, 2000.

Bridgman, Helen Bartlett. *Within My Horizon*. Boston: Small, Maynard and Company, 1920.

Burke, Peter. *Popular Culture in Early Modern Europe*. 3rd ed. Burlington, Vt.: Ashgate, 2009.

Caldwell, Wilber W. *Cynicism and the Evolution of the American Dream*. Washington D.C.: Potomac, 2006.

Charles, Barbara Fahs, and Robert Staples. *Dream of Santa: Haddon Sundblom's Vision*. Alexandria, Va.: Staples and Charles, 1992.

Coca-Cola Collectible Santas. Dallas: Beckett, 2000.

Cohen, Lizabeth. *A Consumers' Republic: The Politics of Mass Consumption in Postwar America*. New York: Alfred A. Knopf, 2003.

Connelly, Mark, ed. *Christmas at the Movies: Images of Christmas in American, British and European Cinema*. New York: I. B. Tauris, 2000.

Coontz, Stephanie. *The Way We Never Were: American Families and the Nostalgia Trap*. New York: Basic Books, 1992.

Cross, Gary S. *The Cute and the Cool: Wondrous Innocence and Modern American Children's Culture*. New York: Oxford University Press, 2004.

Davis, Fred. *Yearning for Yesterday: A Sociology of Nostalgia*. New York: Free Press, 1979.

deChant, Dell. *The Sacred Santa: Religious Dimensions of Consumer Culture*. Eugene, Ore.: Wipf and Stock, 2002.

Diamond, Edwin. "Singing Those Christmas Holiday Blues." *New Yorker Magazine*, December 17, 1967, 32–33, 35–39.
Dickens, Charles. *A Christmas Carol*. London: Chapman and Hall, 1843. Reprint, New York: Dover, 1991.
Dorson, Richard M. "Yuletide Gift-Givers." Reprinted in *The Abbott Christmas Book*. Garden City, N.J.: Doubleday, 1960.
Dundes, Alan. *Christmas as a Reflection of American Culture*. Privately printed, 1970.
Ennis, Philip H. *The Seventh Stream: The Emergence of Rocknroll in American Popular Music*. Middletown, Conn.: Wesleyan University Press, 1992.
Evans, G. S. "Consumerism in the USA: A Nation of Junkies?" *Synthesis/Regeneration* 57 (Winter 2012): 23–26.
Forbes, Bruce David. *Christmas: A Candid History*. Berkeley: University of California Press, 2007.
Freinkel, Susan. *American Chestnut: The Life, Death, and Rebirth of a Perfect Tree*. Berkeley: University of California Press, 2007.
Gardner, Martin. *The Annotated Night Before Christmas: A Collection of Sequels, Parodies, and Imitations of Clement Moore's Immortal Ballad about Santa Claus*. New York: Simon and Schuster, 1991.
Hall, Dennis R. "The Venereal Confronts the Venerable: 'Playboy' on Christmas." *Journal of American Culture* 7, no. 4 (Winter 1984): 63–68.
Hearn, Michael Patrick. *The Annotated Christmas Carol: A Christmas Carol in Prose*. New York: W. W. Norton, 2004.
Highet, Gilbert. *The Anatomy of Satire*. Princeton, N.J.: Princeton University Press, 1962.
Hirschman, Elizabeth C., ed. *Interpretive Consumer Research*. Provo, Utah: Association for Consumer Research, 1989.
Hollis, Tim. *Christmas Wishes: A Catalog of Vintage Holiday Treats & Treasures*. Mechanicsburg, Pa.: Stackpole, 2010.
Horsley, Richard, and James Tracy, eds. *Christmas Unwrapped: Consumerism, Christ, and Culture*. Harrisburg, Pa.: Trinity Press International, 2001.
I'll Be Home for Christmas: The Library of Congress Revisits the Spirit of Christmas During World War II. New York: Delacorte Press, 1999.
Jezer, Marty. *The Dark Ages: Life in the United States 1945–1960*. Boston: South End Press, 1982.
Kinser, Samuel. *Carnival, American Style: Mardi Gras at New Orleans and Mobile*. Chicago: University of Chicago Press, 1990.
Lingeman, Richard R. *Don't You Know There's a War On? The American Home Front, 1941–1945*. New York: G. P. Putnam's Sons, 1970. Reprint, New York: Thunder's Mouth, 2003.

Lowe, Scott C., ed. *Christmas—Philosophy for Everyone: Better Than a Lump of Coal*. Malden, Mass.: Wiley-Blackwell, 2010.
Marling, Karal Ann. *Merry Christmas! Celebrating America's Greatest Holiday*. Cambridge, Mass.: Harvard University Press, 2000.
Marsh, Dave, and Steve Propes. *Merry Christmas, Baby: Holiday Music from Bing to Sting*. New York: Little, Brown, and Company, 1993.
Martell, Joanne, ed. *American Christmases: Firsthand Accounts of Holiday Happenings from Early Days to Modern Times*. Winston-Salem, N.C.: John F. Blair, 2005.
Martin, Linda, and Kerry Segrave. *Anti-Rock: The Opposition to Rock 'n' Roll*. New York: Da Capo, 1993.
McGovern, Charles F. *Sold American: Consumption and Citizenship, 1890–1945*. Chapel Hill: University of North Carolina Press, 2006.
McLuhan, Marshall. *The Mechanical Bride*. New York: Vanguard, 1951.
Mendelson, Lee (with Bill Melendez). *A Charlie Brown Christmas: The Making of a Tradition*. New York: Harper Resource, 2000.
Menendez, Albert J., and Shirley C. Menendez. *Christmas Songs Made in America: Favorite Holiday Melodies and the Stories of Their Origins*. Nashville: Cumberland House, 1999.
Miller, Daniel, ed. *Unwrapping Christmas*. New York: Oxford University Press, 1993.
Mintz, Steven, and Susan Kellogg. *Domestic Revolutions: A Social History of American Family Life*. New York: Free Press, 1987.
Morris, Lloyd. *Postscript to Yesterday: American Life and Thought 1896/1946*. New York: Harper Colophon, 1965.
Moses, Grandma. *Grandma Moses: My Life's Story*. New York: Harper and Brothers, 1952.
Nissenbaum, Stephen. *The Battle for Christmas: A Cultural History of America's Most Cherished Holiday*. New York: Vintage, 1996.
Otfinoski, Steve. *The Golden Age of Novelty Songs*. New York: Billboard, 2000.
Pendergrast, Mark. *For God, Country, and Coca-Cola: The Unauthorized History of the Great American Soft Drink and the Company That Makes It*. New York: Charles Scribner's Sons, 1993.
Pleck, Elizabeth H. *Celebrating the Family: Ethnicity, Consumer Culture, and Family Rituals*. Cambridge, Mass.: Harvard University Press, 2000.
Qutb, Sayyid. "America I Have Seen." In *America in an Arab Mirror: Images of America in Arabic Travel Literature*, ed. Kamal Abdel-Malek, 9–28. New York: Palgrave Macmillan, 2000.
Restad, Penne L. *Christmas in America: A History*. New York: Oxford University Press, 1995.

Rosen, Jody. *White Christmas: The Story of an American Song*. New York: Scribner, 2002.

Rosenthal, Norman E. *Winter Blues: Seasonal Affective Disorder: What It Is and How to Overcome It*, rev. ed. New York: Guildford, 1998.

Scheurer, Timothy E., ed. *The Nineteenth Century Tin Pan Alley*. Vol. 1 of *American Popular Music*. Bowling Green, Ohio: Bowling Green State University Popular Press, 1989.

Schmidt, Leigh Eric. *Consumer Rites: The Buying and Selling of American Holidays*. Princeton, N.J.: Princeton, 1995.

Seeley, Mary Evans. *Season's Greetings from the White House*. Tampa, Fla.: Presidential Christmas Corporation, 1998.

Studwell, William. *The Christmas Carol Reader*. Binghamton, N.Y.: Haworth, 1995.

Tarkington, Booth. *The Magnificent Ambersons*. New York: Grosset and Dunlap, 1918.

Tindall, George Brown. *America: A Narrative History*. New York: W. W. Norton, 1984.

Twitchell, James B. *Adcult USA: The Triumph of Advertising in American Culture*. New York: Columbia University Press, 1996.

Waggoner, Susan. *It's a Wonderful Christmas: The Best of the Holidays 1940–1965*. New York: Stewart, Tabori and Chang, 2004.

Waits, William B. *The Modern Christmas in America: A Cultural History of Gift Giving*. New York: New York University Press, 1993.

Whitburn, Joel. *Christmas in the Charts: 1920–2004*. New York: Billboard, 2004.

Whiteley, Sheila, ed. *Christmas, Ideology and Popular Culture*. Edinburgh: Edinburgh University Press, 2008.

Wigginton, Eliot, and Margie Bennett, eds. *Foxfire 9*. New York: Doubleday, 1986.

Yes, Virginia, There Is a Santa Claus: Cartoons from Playboy. Chicago: Playboy, 1971.

Zinsser, William. *Easy to Remember: The Great American Songwriters and Their Songs*. Jaffrey, N.H.: David R. Godine, 2001.

Index

RONALD D. LANKFORD JR. is an independent scholar whose writing focuses on the cultural history of American popular music. His first book, *Folk Music USA,* was published by Schirmer in 2005; his second book, *Women Singer-Songwriters in Rock,* was published by Scarecrow Press in 2010. Lankford currently lives with his wife, Elizabeth, and nine cats in Appomattox, Virginia.

The University Press of Florida is the scholarly publishing agency for the State University System of Florida, comprising Florida A&M University, Florida Atlantic University, Florida Gulf Coast University, Florida International University, Florida State University, New College of Florida, University of Central Florida, University of Florida, University of North Florida, University of South Florida, and University of West Florida.